Endorsements

Each day, we are invited to gain life wisdom through living. While many of Michelle's circumstances and experiences might be unique to her story, her thoughts and processes can find place in our lives, as well. And God's presence and words are meant to ring in our ears, too. Thank you, Michelle, for putting down on paper what has been woven into your very being.

Marilyn Peters – beloved ragamuffin child of God

Beautiful vulnerability! I celebrate Michelle and the realization of a dream to write this book. What an accomplishment! What a story! Deep and serious. Light and silly. Wouldn't it be wonderful if we all shared our stories and were seen and known like Michelle by her dear friend, Mama, from The Land of Transformation? Michelle says, "This book isn't for everyone." I disagree.

Jimm Derksen, Vice President of the Soul Care Institute

In the tradition of Saint Augustine of Hippo's Confessions, Michelle Martin has made herself vulnerable and exposed through writing that is part memoir, prayer, psychology, and raw conversations with her own soul. She grapples with her "physical uniqueness" that at one time would have been characterized as a crippling handicap instead of marking her as "differently abled" with "super powers." Her journey of self-discovery follows both Road to Emmaus "ohs" and Road to Damascus "Ahhs." Traveling mercies, dear reader.

John Helt, author of *Lydia Hosto Niebuhr: The Buried History of an Evangelical Matriarch*

In reference to our spiritual journeys, we often say that we move from clarity to clarity. Michelle's story turns from hardship to hardship. Her transparency in sharing about these difficulties is refreshing. This unflinching look at childhood, relationships, grief, and the church will have you questioning how your actions, or inactions, ripple into the world. You may resonate with some experiences, you may be offended by others... and rightly so! I have been challenged to assess my impact on the world, and you will be too.

Timothy Zehr - Spiritual Director, Associate Pastor at Sunnyside Mennonite Church

Martin gives fair warning in her introduction that she is about to take the reader on a journey and that this journey might prove disturbing to some readers. But what a journey it is. Emotional vulnerability and honesty in telling a life story describe Martin's book in a nutshell. Exploring themes like shame, guilt and personal agency, the author leads the reader into emotional and theological reflection. I love how she openly explores the differences between shame and guilt within the framework of Western and Jewish theology. Through narration and reflection, Martin demonstrates remarkable insights into her inner life, powerfully introspective, without the self-focus that can make such a gift self-centered. Touching on doubts, mental health, marriage, and grief, she also delves into Christian Nationalism, American history (yes the ugly bits as well), bad church experiences, and COVID. Martin navigates the minefield of dearly guarded beliefs with a dignity and honesty that is refreshing and endearing.

Leon Miller - Pastor, counselor, one acquainted with grief

I am privileged to have known Michelle for the last 20 or so years. In this brave telling of her story, Michelle discloses that she lacks in confidence. I can tell you, however, that she certainly doesn't lack courage. In Michelle's book, she invites us into her struggles, and by doing so she gives us permission to honestly engage our own.

Jenny Gehman, author of *Little Life Words: 60 Meditations to Soothe, Center, and Strengthen Your Soul*

In this book, Michelle brings us along on the beautiful, deep path of her life. She has dug deeply into her own understanding of living and what that means for the earnest Christian. Continually drawing on her knowledge of who God is and how God relates to her through her unique being. She has learned to look through the pain and suffering to see the beauty and depth of love that God has for her, and she willingly and openly shares that with those who read her story. She is neither pretentious nor a "know it all" but generously shares of herself, her journey, and her experiences with humility and a passion for making sense of it all. It is a gift that she writes in a way that draws the reader into her life without overburdening the silent participants of her story with blame nor shame. There is healing to be found within this story and these pages.

Rev. H. Jill Hofer

EMBRACING SMALL
BEGINNINGS

Embracing Small Beginnings

My Journey From Chaos to Clarity

Michelle Martin

SANTOS BOOKS
EVERY STORY SACRED

First Printing, 2025

Published by Santos Books, Elizabethtown, PA 17022

ISBN: 979-8-9994186-8-5

Contents

To Lucas:
Thank you for pushing me to be better than I was
yesterday. I wrote this book partly because I want you
to see that with hard work and the Holy Spirit, life is
ultimately beautiful and absolutely worth living. I love
you!

Acknowledgments

First and foremost, thank You Jesus, for Your strength, wisdom, insight, and humor in my life. Thank You for walking with me and for reminding me that it is out of the nature of rest that our life's work is to be completed.

To Keith - May the LORD bless you and keep you...and all the other good stuff. We joke about our stubbornness, but it's honestly brought us far. Thanks for being stubbornly committed to me. I love you!

To the people who shepherded us at various points through the crazy times - Jill, Tom and Linda, Adam, Jack, and members from the Soul Care Institute team - Jimm, Kaylene, and Katy. You have been "Jesus with skin on" through your kindness, gentleness, and wisdom. Thank you!

To the people who broke through a roof to lower us to Jesus - Jess and Chuny, Carla, Age, Amy, Kate, Jess R, our parents. Thanks for showing up in practical ways and for listening and letting me vent. It means a lot!

To my proofreader, Cindy - I have to give you credit for my writing. All those years ago in Tandem 2, you helped mold my writing style and encouraged me every step of the way. It was truly an honor to have your expertise shape my book. Thank you!

To my copyeditor, Sharon - Over the years, I've learned a lot from you about love, kindness, and inclusion of everyone, and these lessons still impact my everyday life. Thank you for your questions and observations about my book; they helped me go more in-depth and encouraged me that the readers want to know more, not less!

Foreword

"God is okay with who you are," is Michelle Martin's message. Her book *Embracing Small Beginnings: My Journey from Chaos to Clarity* is a refreshing read of God's love and embrace of humanity. Michelle, a friend since her early college days and sister in the Lord, is a passionate woman of Mennonite heritage. A woman who is Holy Spirit-filled, transparent, emotionally honest, and not afraid to dialogue with God on life's controversial topics: parenting with her physical uniqueness, her husband's mental health concerns, and the church's hypocrisy and betrayal of its fundamental calling in light of Christian Nationalism. It is evident from her understanding of biblical texts and her writing that Jesus loves and accepts her unconditionally. Michelle has not allowed her traditional Mennonite community to undermine this reality nor hinder her from pursuing God whole-heartedly. Born with hydrocephalus (fluid on the brain), Michelle takes on life's challenges with integrity and zest. She is empathic. Transparent. Vulnerable. Michelle's relationship with Jesus is insightful and intensely personal.

Reading Michelle's book will encourage you to get real with God. Honest with God, at the deepest level of one's being. In the inner space, one tends to deny one's feelings, thoughts, and struggles. One is inclined to ignore those inner struggles because of fear and rejection of friends, of church rebuttals, and shaming. These topics are struggles simply because one knows they cannot be overlooked if one desires an authentic encounter with God and true inner peace. I found her prayer dialogue with Jesus to be a creative, unique way to process faith and life spiritually. The prayer reflects a genuinely open and trusting relationship she has cultivated with Jesus over the years.

If you want a living example of a dynamic relationship with Jesus, I highly recommend *Embracing Small Beginnings: My Journey from Chaos to Clarity*. As you read Michelle's book, I invite you to journal and pray with Jesus about your feelings, thoughts, and struggles in life, faith, and church. Michelle has led by example by saying that God loves you as you are. You can bring all your questions, doubts, and faults to Him. He is listening and ready to engage with your life with love, acceptance, and open arms.

Jack Scandrett, retired Mennonite Pastor

Introduction: "Spicy Christian Literature"

This book isn't for everyone. I talk about religion, politics, parenting, missionary strategy, among other things. Everyone will get upset with me at one point or another in this book. A friend asked if this book is a "diss track" or a soapbox, of sorts. I think that's an accurate description.

Shame and vulnerability researcher Brene Brown has a list of values on her website[1]. No value is more or less important, but we all have values that explain why we lead life the way we do. It didn't take me long to pick my top two values: honesty and justice. I am an open book, and I say what I mean and mean what I say. I also have a deep sense of fairness and yearn to help everyone get what they need - and then some! Gandhi once said "Live simply, so others may simply live." I try to model my life after that quote.

Based on the way a lot of my relationships have gone over the last five years, *I'm* not for everyone. The way I have lived out these two values in my life has almost been too literal for some people. For some people, I could have toned myself down. I could have kept some things to myself. I could have cared less. I could have turned a blind eye to some things.

But I can't do any of that. I'm a pot stirrer by nature. I sense when something is off and try to make it right again. Author Jamie Wright has talked about being a "spiritual laxative," trying to move the waste in the Church along, so better and healthier sustenance can come take its place. I felt that in my soul. I empathize with the prophet Jeremiah when he says in Jeremiah 20 that he's frustrated with the calling God has placed on his life. However, if Jeremiah doesn't fulfill the calling, it will eat him up inside. I'm between a rock and a hard place.

I am far from perfect and my messy imperfection continually brings me back to this – the conviction that Jesus is for the underdogs. Jesus is for those who are in last place. Jesus is for the weak, the vulnerable, and the outcasts.

This book tells my story. I came into the world as an underdog, and now my mission is to speak up for all the underdogs I can.

If this book ruffles your feathers, I don't want you to imagine me pointing my finger at you and laughing. I want you to picture me extending my hand towards you in an invitation to wrestle. To wrestle with your past, your convictions, and the way you lead life, ultimately to discover why my words have an effect on your feathers in the first place. In my wrestling with Jesus lately, He often asks me this question that pops up later in the book: "Why do you care so strongly about how other people carry themselves?" In Scripture, we are only told to control ourselves, never to control another. May His question be a breather for you rather than another burden to carry.

This book is for

The pot stirrers

The spiritual laxatives

The vulnerable - in any capacity

The doubters

The deconstructors

The questioners

The whistle blowers

The advocates - in any and all forms

You are not crazy. You can ignore all the gaslighters and trust that your heart is beating for the right things. You are seen. You are known. You are LOVED. Rest in that knowledge and change the world with the power it gives you.

[1] Brown, Brene. 2022. "Living into our Values." Brene Brown. 2022. https://brenebrown.com/resources/living-into-our-values/.

One

It's a Good Day to Talk about Feelings

I am the youngest of three siblings. As a mom of one child, I can't imagine three. I've heard people say that parents become more lax with each additional child, and that makes perfect sense. Parents have to survive somehow.

My mom has said that I developed slowly in my first year of life. I met milestones but took my time, and since my sister and brother also developed at slower rates, my parents assumed this was all normal. It wasn't until I needed to go to the doctor for a simple ear infection that my parents realized something was amiss. My usual doctor wasn't in, so I saw someone new. I think he was relatively new to the practice, and he was a boisterous Italian with an endearing accent. However, when it was time to get down to business, he was ready. This appointment was no exception. Right away, he said, "Her head is too big, and this needs to get checked out."

That doctor saved my life.

As it turns out, my other doctor suspected something was amiss, but he never informed my parents of his concerns. As my mom updated his receptionist on my diagnosis, the receptionist revealed the

3

news. As bizarre as it sounds, it seems like the doctor wanted to give my parents the responsibility of saying there was a problem while he stayed in contented silence. Even as I type this, I have to take deep breaths and say audibly that I forgive this doctor. What a coward. Who does that? Who places that kind of burden on a baby's parents? I have told my parents numerous times that I do not blame them, that it is not their fault. I think about it a lot and always ask God to wipe away whatever residue is left from that wound.

I was diagnosed with Hydrocephalus - fluid on the brain. My bigger head size was a result of fluid buildup. We all have fluid on our brains, but it can typically drain out on its own. Hydrocephalus occurs when the fluid is stuck inside. The most common solution is a shunt (tube) that drains the fluid. I had the surgery at 8 months old, and the surgeons said that it would need to be lengthened every two years. At the original writing of this chapter, my shunt just turned 37 years old - no adjustments, no replacements needed. Several years after the surgery, they discovered that there is enough shunt in me to grow to be six feet tall! I'm 5'2", so that will never happen!

Every time this anniversary comes around, I am reminded that I am walking on holy ground every day. My story is not everyone's story. People die from this condition. I have plenty of other challenges in life, but thankfully, the life of my shunt hasn't been one of them.

If I just had Hydrocephalus, I could blend in more with the world. It can be an invisible condition; people can't always tell just by looking at the person. However, as life would have it, I stood out instead.

****

If I had been diagnosed with Hydrocephalus soon after birth, I may not have had any further complications. However, since the Hydrocephalus went undetected for eight months, enough damage occurred for a mild case of Cerebral Palsy to develop. Just my left side is affected, but it's been enough to be life-altering.

I compare my left hand to a mitten. I can use the hand, but the fingers don't cooperate. During different speaking engagements, I would often invite people to tie their shoes with a mitten on one hand. As the participants have all experienced, it doesn't work too well.

In some ways, I'm glad I've had this condition since infancy because I don't know what I'm missing. I don't know what it's like to live life two-handed. Recently, my mom found some of my preschool documents. "Preschool" for me meant physical and occupational therapy starting at age one because my parents wanted to give me all the support possible. I really appreciate that now, but back then...

I hated it. I hated all the therapy.

One particular paragraph in the documents stuck out to me. I was three-ish and in a setting with kids of various developmental delays. The therapist wrote that I disliked being singled out for therapy and wouldn't calm down until the therapist asked another girl to join me. It was also apparent to me that the other girl could do more physical things than I could. I don't remember how I felt in that exact moment from the paragraph, but I've had other experiences where it was blatantly obvious that I was developmentally delayed, and I never felt good. I felt ashamed and less than, and I had also had a fear of what the future might hold for me.

I do have a memory of a therapy session where I felt vindicated. I was four, and it was a joint session with a boy who also had Cerebral Palsy. That day, he and I were having none of it. Anything the therapist asked of us, we refused. We saw the mounting frustration in our parents and therapist, an observation that only encouraged us more.

Of course, I empathize with the adults now. Our moms only wanted the best for us, and the therapist was just trying to do her job. However, this is a core memory because it shows me that I would do anything to maintain some semblance of control in my life. Even if the control looked like chaos on the outside.

Don't we all want control of our lives? As a mom, I can definitely say, "YES." My son wants to demonstrate that he has agency - the capability to exert power over a situation - and that's extremely important. Please understand, having agency doesn't mean that life will go exactly the way we want. Having agency means that, to some extent, we can make life happen FOR us instead of TO us. Having agency allows us to live life intentionally.

I'm sure my mom would say I had plenty of moments as a toddler where I put my agency on display, but that therapy session sticks out to me because it's my first memory of standing up for myself. And there were many more to come.

****

Since my birthday is in August, my parents decided to wait until I was six to send me to school. With my physical uniqueness, they figured it best to give me the gift of time. It was honestly one of the best gifts they have ever given me.

My kindergarten teacher may have been a good teacher for...older kids, young adults, maybe? But for 5- and 6-year-olds? I try to have compassion for her and be empathetic towards her situation, but Come. On. If you know working with little kids isn't your strength, don't do it! Some evidence to back up my claim is that she sent my friend to the principal's office for a minor incident - my friend pinched someone who was interfering with her schoolwork. That consequence was completely unnecessary.

My old friend "agency" was a regular companion in kindergarten. Agency often manifested itself in tears. Every single day. I needed to be noticed somehow because I didn't feel emotionally safe. I didn't feel supported. I was being confronted daily with the fact that I truly was physically unique and had no educator by my side to help me process what that looks like in school. I had occupational therapists come and go in the classroom to provide some ways to physically support me, but my main teacher was emotionally absent.

I have to wonder if kindergarten was a trigger for my mind and body. Was I transported back to infancy when a qualified professional should have stepped up and did not, and I was left with the consequences of his negligence? Was I starting to notice a pattern of indifference in adults where they actually had the power to have a positive impact and chose not to? Did my agency stem from the sobering fact that, to some extent, I had to take my life in my own hands at the age of 6?

I do remember being able to learn the material in kindergarten, though. I really caught on to reading, which turned into a lifelong passion. OK, so maybe she was a good teacher who just lacked nurturing skills. I simply felt a constant emotional burden but never knew what it was. Let's put a pin in that.

I remember assignments stressing me out even back then. For one assignment on the alphabet, we had to cut and paste pictures from magazines or newspapers. Where was I going to find a picture of something starting with 'x?' I hated cutting things out! What is the point of it all?!' (Update: I still cut like a kindergartner at times! My 10th-grade Biology teacher even asked me how I passed kindergarten with my low skill level in this area! That was all meant in jest, of course.)

One day, I had to leave class to count to 100 with an aide in the hallway. I wasn't worried about the task. I was worried that I would miss something in class. My mom was working with another student in the hallway and remembers me counting in between gulping sobs. My ever-faithful friend - agency. Things were not OK. Afterwards, my teacher asked if I cried while counting, and I lied and said "no." I was awful at lying (still am!), but I wanted to stick it to her somehow. I wanted to preserve my six-year-old dignity.

Somehow, I survived that year and first grade, as well. It was not until second grade that I realized adults can actually like teaching.

And, during third grade, I began to have revelations about myself, but we'll come back to that in a bit.

****

I've discussed my physical uniqueness and the chaos it caused in my early years. Let's talk about feelings now. One of my favorite shirts says, "It's a good day to talk about feelings." I truly believe that's every day. I'm not sure why God created me to be both physically unique as well as highly sensitive emotionally, because that combination has given a lot of Mennonites headaches! Mennonites, who form a Christian denomination by the same name, tend to present a stoic front to the world; everything is OK all of the time, and even when it's not, it's important to just move on. My physical uniqueness showed everyone around me that I wasn't the typical definition of "fine." I couldn't "move on" from my way of being, so perhaps my physical uniqueness influences my highly sensitive nature. Or it could be God just nudging me to trust that He's in the mystery.

I heard somewhere that excitement and anxiety are two sides of the same coin. I felt that deeply and found that it explained a lot about my experiences. I think excitement is innocent enough; it exhibits the belief that everything will go well. Excitement is like a naive little child who is looking forward to a birthday party. Anxiety comes along as the all-knowing mother who knows what work has to go into the party. Anxiety wants everything to go well but feels like it has to control every aspect for everything to go well. Anxiety pumps excitement's brakes a bit, and it causes a lot of feelings of tension. Growing up, I tended to have stomach aches leading up to an event I anticipated, and I think the feeling was the result of excitement and anxiety meeting up.

Another contributing factor is that I am an idealist, so it has been imperative to me that the outcome of any event be favorable. I love having something to look forward to, but if my expectations aren't exactly met, it's tough to reconcile my emotions with reality.

As a child, I sometimes hid before guests came over. I was excited for them to come; I just had this urge to hide. I never knew why. My son does this now, and I finally get it. The excitement is present, but there is also anxiety. Are my expectations going to be met? Is my excitement worth it? I'll come out when I'm ready, when I feel in control of myself and the situation.

What if I never feel "in control" of the situation, though? I remember when my family came to visit me during my year in Germany after college. I was very excited to see them. I hadn't seen them in months, and I was also dealing with some weird back pain that we couldn't find the cause of. Secretly, I couldn't wait to be cared for. When they finally came, I felt the clock immediately start to tick towards their return home. I couldn't stop time, nor could I stop my anxiety. We had a good time, but anxiety did cast a real shadow.

The same thing happened on my honeymoon. Of course, I was excited, but anxiety tagged along like an unwanted guest. I wasn't sure why it happened. We had some great moments, such as going to an improv show (that we still quote to this day!), eating some great lobster, and seeing a humpback whale jump completely out of the water. However, I still felt this undercurrent of anxiety. I'm sure some of it was normal; I had just committed to being with someone for my entire life after all. I thought my anxiety would taper off after we arrived home, but no. There was a motorcycle event near our house that Sunday, and the constant revving of motors outside our house exacerbated my anxiety and exhaustion from the honeymoon. I was a wreck. I'm sure Keith was thinking, "The rest of my life, huh?"

Since realizing that excitement and anxiety are so closely related, I have been able to work on myself a bit. I let myself get excited, and I also give myself a pep talk. I can't have perfect expectations because there are no perfect people - me being the key person! There are things I can control, and while I can't control situations, I can control my response. When I know my response won't be ideal, I can give myself grace to leave the situation.

****

I've heard of the term 'terminally unique,' a tongue-in-cheek term used to describe someone who thinks they are different from others in various areas of life. It's so tempting for me to use that term for myself because I really am different from people in my area. If I asked people I grew up with if they knew someone else who was both emotionally intense as well as physically unique, most of them would say I am the only person like that in their lives. I don't want to use that term as an excuse and demand that I be treated as though I were fragile, but I do want people to acknowledge that we have led different lives. My situation has required me to jump through hoops others haven't had to.

I've read a number of books and listened to lots of podcasts, and I've learned that if you're not of a certain gender, race, religion, physical ability, mental ability, socioeconomic status...you're lesser than.

This 'lesser than' status is on purpose. I used to think it was just because of living in a "fallen world," but from all that I've listened to and read, it has become blatantly clear that these systems are intentional. They are designed specifically to churn out the results they get.

I am incredibly privileged, and I can check off several of those boxes that tell the world to treat me well. However, my physical uniqueness (and my highly sensitive nature, to an extent) can make people uncomfortable. It wasn't until writing the very first draft of this chapter that it hit me. The emotional burden I felt in kindergarten was people's discomfort of me. The way I present myself to the world - my physical and emotional vulnerabilities - makes people aware that I don't exactly fit the bill of what they call "normal." My very presence in people's lives presents them with a challenge to step out of their "normal" box and engage with me in a way that might make their vulnerabilities apparent, as well.

When interacting with others in ways where my physical uniqueness is apparent, I know people don't want to say or do the wrong thing. They don't want to offend me. I get that, and I appreciate that. But in doing and saying nothing, they put the emotional burden of their discomfort on me. Some people may be thinking, "You're so high maintenance, Michelle!" Well, let me just give you practical and everyday examples that friends have gifted me with over the years:

"Michelle, I know you struggle with higher tables (in a cafe setting), so I made sure to grab us a lower table."

Before spending a day touring Washington DC, "What can I do to make this day as easy as possible for you?"

I had just met someone, and she offered to do my nails. My left hand makes that experience A TASK. She didn't mind and said she loves challenges. We laughed and bonded, and she is now one of my dearest friends.

All of those examples resulted in me getting choked up because I realized there were some people who willingly carried my burden...only they didn't see it as such. They simply saw it as a part of me that deserved love just as much as the rest of me did.

****

If I could have said to my kindergarten self, "There are people who will accept and love you for who you are," I wonder how I would be different. Granted, I only needed to wait three years to discover this, but three years is a long time.

Thankfully, I started to have success in second grade, and to paraphrase Maya Angelou, I started caring about what teachers knew because I knew how much they cared about me. I entered third grade feeling better about education.

I began to put words to the emotional burden I felt since kindergarten. They came in the form of questions:

Am I the only person like this?

What did I do to deserve this?

What does everyone think of me?

Who can I talk to about this?

It was hard to talk about these questions with my parents. I understand now; they didn't know what to say to me because they didn't receive much moral support or encouragement from others, either. I think the questions I was asking myself were questions they asked themselves, too. But I had to talk to someone.

In third grade, I finally had a teacher who was able to validate my emotional struggles. Mrs. Peachey introduced us to journaling, and when we turned our entries in, we had the option to keep it private or to share with her. I kept my first entry private. I really wrote out my feelings, though. I was angry and confused about something that happened in gym class.

As the weeks passed, I gradually got the sense that I could trust her, so I wrote a vulnerable entry that she had permission to read. Her response put my life on a new trajectory. She thanked me for sharing, and she highlighted strengths she saw in me. She acknowledged my questions while encouraging me to focus on the truth in front of me. I had a lot of people who cared for me. I was capable of excellence. Most importantly, I had worth simply because I was alive.

That encouragement carried me throughout the rest of the year. It even helped me during track and field. I mentioned that gym class wasn't the most exciting place for me, and as I watched the same few people go up on stage to receive one blue ribbon after another, I realized something. I won't be good at everything. I can't be good at everything. I needed to find what I was good at and throw myself into it. I knew academics were my only option, so I dove in.

Mrs. Peachey planted the seed for my love of learning and is the very first reason I am who I am today.

Two

Fire Insurance and/or Love?

I once heard a speaker talk about the different ways we hear from God. Sometimes we experience Him the way Saul did on the road to Damascus - WHOA! We fall off our horses, we are blinded on impact, and are fundamentally changed in an instant. Other times, we experience God the way the disciples did on the road to Emmaus - ohhhh. We pause, our eyes open, and we get enough strength for the day to keep believing, to keep hoping, to keep moving forward.

I resonated a lot with this message. Like me, this speaker, this other Mennonite, wished he had had more WHOA moments in his life - a more exciting testimony, more dramatic Acts-type experiences, more adventure.

Don't get me wrong, I have had my WHOA moments (the reason this book is in existence!), and honestly, they are EXHAUSTING. I truly believe if all we had were WHOA moments, we would never experience rest. I don't know if the shepherds in the Christmas story could have endured being "sore afraid" indefinitely. I read somewhere that the butterfly feelings of a new relationship would cause harm to our bodies if they lasted forever.

We need stability. We need routines. As much as I hate to say it, we need...the mundane.

I grew up in that kind of home. I have parents who are committed to each other, and they were committed to raising my siblings and me in a Christian home. We lacked nothing; looking back, I notice a lot of abundance in my past. I grew up with a lot of privilege, and because of that privilege, I can lead the life I lead today. I'm thankful and am aware that "to whom much is given, much is required".

My family is Swiss-German, and most of my family is stoic. They keep to themselves, and most likely shudder at the thought of me writing a book. "Why do you have to air your dirty laundry?!" In some ways, I am absolutely the black sheep of the family, simply because I have never fit into that lifestyle. I'm loud and passionate, and I wear my heart on my sleeve.

****

At church, the congregants were kind. I have several memories of adults helping me navigate my way in a 2-handed world with humor and grace. The church was also incredibly generous in contributing to my various globe-trotting endeavors.

The leaders and the Sunday School teachers at the church had the greatest of intentions...yet I'm still working at unlearning things I picked up from them. It's not just this particular church; I feel like a lot of the Church in general in the Western world has teachings that say shame is what brings you to God, and shame is what keeps you close to Him. There's a verse in the song 'Jesus Loves Me:'

Jesus loves me when I'm good, when I do the things I should.
Jesus loves me when I'm bad, though it makes Him very sad.

Those lines make me cringe. We shouldn't do things because they make Jesus happy. We should do things because we love Jesus, and out of this love flow the deeds that bless Him.

Brene Brown talks a lot about the definition of *shame* vs. the definition of *guilt*.[1] *Shame* is 'I am bad.' Shame only survives when we stay silent and keep secrets. The way to get rid of shame is to be vulnerable and talk to others. When we learn we're not alone, the shame begins to disappear.

My son has a book that, while talking about anxious feelings, also applies to shame.[2] In the book, the girl starts feeling worry, and the worry presents itself as a little blob. The little girl keeps her worry to herself, and the worry only grows bigger and scarier until it impacts her whole life. One day at the park, she sees a little boy who has a little blob with him. Could he have a worry, too? It's true! As they begin sharing their worries, they notice that their worries fade away to nothing. I think shame is a lot like that blob, and when we bring it out in the open, it has no room to hide. Shame has to disappear in the light.

Brown's definition of *guilt* is, "I did something bad." We get rid of guilt by confessing what we did and by making things right again. Shame likes to linger. Guilt leaves the minute it is dealt with.

In episode 3 of the BEMA podcast[3], the hosts talk about how the Western world views sin versus how the Jewish world views sin. The Western definition of sin is, "I'm bad. The very core of my being is bad, so naturally I am going to do bad things." Essentially, the Western world's definition of sin is the same as Brown's definition of *shame.*

The Jewish definition of sin is, "I did a bad thing. If the next thing I do is the right thing, I will be right with God again." Essentially, sin isn't in us. It is a decision we make, and we don't need to let it trip us up. God can pick us up, dust us off, and we can go on our way again. It's similar to Brown's definition of *guilt.*

It's taken me years to learn that shame is not what should tie us to God. Guilt and conviction should bring us to God, and love is what should help us stay with Him.

****

When I was at my niece's baptism a few years ago, the pastor said something that I wish I would have heard at my baptism. After the service was over, he looked at the group and simply said, "You made a great declaration today, and I just want you to know that you'll probably mess up this afternoon already, and that's OK. God is bigger than your mistakes." I just stood there, wondering how different my teenage Christian walk would have been had I heard those same words at my baptism.

Maybe I wouldn't have been so freaked out by all the End Times literature and doom and gloom talk. Maybe I wouldn't have gone up at every single altar call out of fear that I lost my salvation somewhere along the way. Maybe I could have learned earlier on that "Do not fear" meant that God delights in my humanity, and I can rest in the fact that He's bigger than any mistake I could ever make.

****

As you may imagine, the way I feel about my walk with Christ might ruffle some Mennonites' feathers. While few have spoken to me about it, I have gotten indirect messaging.

I love personality tests of any kind, and the founders of Enneagram[4] would cringe to hear me include their profile into this category. I'm going to do it anyway. Once I completed the assessment, I received a number between 1 and 9. This number showed me wonderful aspects about myself as well as my darker aspects. The profile isn't meant to shame people; it's meant to demonstrate that we are complex beings. I am a Four, and as Ian Morgan Cron puts it, Fours don't FEEL their feelings; Fours ARE their feelings. I felt so seen when I heard that. I cannot count the number of times I have heard from people of influence in my life, "Change your attitude, Michelle!" "Stop being so sensitive; we were just kidding!"

It boils down to, "I'm uncomfortable with how you're feeling right now, and since you caused the discomfort, I'm simply going to place the discomfort on you. You can deal with it." It's exhausting to have to carry other people's burdens, and as I mentioned in Chapter 1, because the burdens were never mine to carry in the first place, I'm slowly learning to place them all down.

Fours tend to wonder why they are so different from everyone else. As a consequence of that, they want to learn everything they can about themselves in the hopes that they can be "normal" like everyone else. Growing up, I didn't feel successful in my attempts to be normal. Because I feel so deeply about all of the things, I felt ashamed when I heard statements like, "Don't trust your feelings; don't follow your heart." I have no choice but to feel. Feelings tell us so much about ourselves, and they always pass if we feel them the whole way through! I always tell my husband that he needs to let me feel my feelings, and then I will come to the same conclusion he does. And we usually are on the same page in the end!

****

My feelings came in handy when I started on the leadership team at my high school Bible study. I was able to lead on some of the mornings and discovered I enjoyed public speaking. I don't remember any of the topics I discussed, but I remember they were varied and covered numerous emotions. I remember some students thanking me for speaking so passionately, and my reply then as it is now was, "There's no other way to be."

My feelings continued to be welcomed when I joined a church on my college's campus. The lead pastor was wonderful, and his sermons had variety that I never experienced before! Before I entered college, I had never heard anyone preach a sermon on Christmas or Easter that had unique modern-day applications. His sermons left me thinking and yearning for more. I also remember how we did Communion. Before I started college, I just experienced Communion as a solemn occasion, which makes sense,...but it left me bored. Communion at this church had a celebratory flare and helped me understand why we even have this ritual in the first place.

The pastor at my college church welcomed relationship with all of us. It was a new reality for me because I just had superficial relationships with pastors at my home church. Once I realized this pastor was open to talk, I let him have it (in a good way, of course)! Looking back, I cringe at the long emails I sent him, but he appreciated them. He said he wished more students would be that open with him. I met with him once a month to talk more about those emails, and he was so patient, understanding, and insightful. He helped me through several tough times.

This pastor also grew up Mennonite, and he spoke to me a lot about his transition from legalism to a thriving relationship with Jesus. One thing he said to me that I still live by is, in effect, "If something in a relationship causes me to have to choose between truth or grace, I'm choosing grace." Of course, truth is important, but I believe that God will have compassion on nuanced differences in theology more than He will if we don't show grace. Jesus calls us to love God and to love people, and if we look at 1 Corinthians 13, love says nothing about the receiver. It says only what is required of the giver.

****

A year or so after college graduation, I had a vision of Jesus that has stuck with me since then. The vision brought to mind the story of separating the sheep from the goats. Growing up, I always felt a bit of pride when I heard the story. We are the sheep, and Jesus is loudly telling the goats that He's never known them. In stark contrast, this vision showed me that Jesus was weeping, barely able to get the words out. And maybe Matthew didn't hear this when he wrote the gospel, but after Jesus spoke, "I never knew you," He said barely above a whisper, "But I wanted so badly to know you."

I'll get into this later, but I feel like the Western Church runs away from humility and runs straight into the arms of hubris - a dangerous overconfidence. A dangerous overconfidence in what the future holds and in our ability, to make that future happen. A dangerous overconfidence that we also are the Way, the Truth, and the Life to the world, instead of Jesus alone. This hubris has turned us into vigilantes for Jesus.

This hubris is not really surprising, considering US history is full of conquest and victory. Of course, it's going to show up in our theology and worship music. We're too busy worshiping the Jesus to come - King Jesus - that we forget the Jesus born in a manger - God with us. Yes, victory will be ours at some point (WHOA!), but lately, I've just been desiring the God who walks with me in the everyday, the monotony, the mundane (ohhhh).

NOTES

[1] Empowering Insights. 2025. "Shame vs. Guilt | the Difference That Changes Everything | Brené Brown Motivation." YouTube. January 28, 2025. https://www.youtube.com/watch?v=k4i60xcrIvQ.

[2] Percival, Tom. 2020. *Ruby Finds a Worry.* S.L.: Bloomsbury USA.

[3] Solomon, Marty. "Master the Beast." Produced by Brent Billings. *BEMA Podcast.* September 22, 2016. Podcast, 26:27. https://www.bemadiscipleship.com/3

[4] The Enneagram Institute. 2014. "How the Enneagram System Works." The Enneagram Institute. 2014. https://www.enneagramin-stitute.com/how-the-enneagram-system-works/.

Three

When "Never" Becomes Reality

I spent all of Chapter 2 highlighting the "ohhhh" way of experiencing God. This chapter is about a "WHOA" period in my life.

There's a saying: "Never say never," a saying that is eerily accurate. Whenever I've said "never," it has proven to be a challenge to God. A good challenge for sure, because the ways in which He has redeemed my "nevers" have been life-altering.

I was preparing to go to Germany with a mission agency after graduating from college, and there were various events to prepare me to serve with this agency. At one of the events in 2008, the presenter said that wherever God calls us, we will feel a love for that group of people. I remember thinking about a group of people, and I will simply call their homeland *The Land of Transformation.* Though in 2008, I didn't consider it as such. I remember thinking, "I'm sure those people are great, but I'm thankful lots of people go there because I. DON'T. WANT. TO."

I shake my head at that ridiculous memory.

In June of 2011, I had my first ever burning bush moment. I was in the car singing along to the songs on the radio. One song ended, and the Christian radio equivalent of ads came on. All of a sudden, I heard this cheesy announcer-voice: "Help kids in [The Land of Transformation] with Hydrocephalus!" It was hard to stay focused on driving at that time. No one ever talks about Hydrocephalus! As soon as I could, I logged on to the website mentioned.

That was the first time I ever saw the woman I will simply call "Mama." That's who she became to me.

Mama, a native of this country, worked with an organization that provides life-changing, sometimes life-saving surgeries around the world. At the hospital in this particular country, the staff specifically works with babies and children who have Hydrocephalus and Spina Bifida. In the video, Mama shared that many babies are born fine, but they develop Hydrocephalus as a result of infection.

Let's empathize with these families here. The mothers, often miles away from any medical care whatsoever, give birth to beautiful, healthy babies. Over time, though, they notice the baby's head growing in size due to fluid build up...and it looks scary. Superstition often reigns supreme in their clans, and many clan chiefs believe there is demonic involvement in these events. The solution is simple...and awful. The mothers are forced to drown their children. It is believed that the clan is then cleansed from whatever curse was brought on by the baby.

Um...what? I couldn't just sit there and go on with life, pretending that things were normal. Could I?

"Want to go to [The Land of Transformation]?" God asked me. "Absolutely not!" I retorted.

But the seeds were planted, and the wheels started turning. God had spoken to me through that burning bush disguised in a radio ad, inviting me to take my shoes off and to accept His invitation to do something I said I'd never do. How was I going to respond?

****

I couldn't get this thought out of my head, so around Christmas time in 2011, I checked out the website to see if there were any short-term trips planned for the following summer. I told God, "It has to be a general trip; I would be useless on a medical trip." He met His end of the deal; there was a general trip the following summer!

Gulp

I applied right away. Some might say it was a rash decision, but it really wasn't. Over the last six months, I had been thinking, analyzing, and praying about the idea of a trip to The Land of Transformation...when I had zero desire to go just a year prior.

I got a call from one of the team leaders in the new year. She was excited about my story and eagerly offered me a spot on the team. Here goes nothing, or was it...everything?

****

I remember someone saying, "Stop believing Satan is after you; that's arrogant. He's after more important people, like world leaders. If anything is after you, it's lesser demons." Over the years, my faith has evolved to the point where I hesitate to call things persecution or opposition. I've found it more helpful - healthier, even - to just chalk things up to life being imperfect.

Whatever the theology, the time leading up to this trip was interesting. My employers said they would have to let me go if I went on the trip because three weeks off was a big deal. Was I seriously putting my job on the line for a place I never wanted to go to? Apparently, yes. Eventually, my employers came around and said I could still work there.

The flight out was scheduled for the end of June, and in May, I started feeling pain around my shunt. It was the first time in years, and I was so frustrated. The mission organization said that while I would be fine at the hospital, they were concerned about outreach, because we would be out in the middle of nowhere. They needed to see a note from my neurologist.

I hadn't seen a neurologist since I was a child because I was living according to the motto, "If it's not broken, don't fix it." I had to quickly find one and make an appointment. Long story short, the pain eventually subsided, the neurologist wrote the note, and I was free to go.

While waiting for the first leg of my journey at the airport, I was in a state of mild denial. I couldn't believe I was going to this country instead of Germany. Germany was my calling, not here! I felt my feet turning cold in the proverbial sense. I had jumped off the cliff, but was I going to be successful, or was this endeavor going to end in one big splat?

****

My teammate and I landed for our 11-hour layover, and we headed to the designated meeting spot to join the rest of our group.

I didn't sleep a wink on the first flight, and as we joined the rest of the group, it was clear my teammates were in the same state I was. As I looked for a place to sit, one of my teammates patted the seat next to her and said to me, "Here, shit." Bleary-eyed, I looked at her, my confused facial expression matching everyone else's. As soon as she realized what she said, we all erupted in laughter. It was the perfect icebreaker. We spent the long layover walking around, getting to know each other, and trying not to fall asleep.

I was a bundle of nerves as we boarded the next flight. I was going further than I had ever gone before. Was I really doing the right thing? I had a window seat, which I enjoy, and thankfully, I was able to get a few hours of sleep. I woke up to the sunrise. On an airplane, thousands of feet up in the air. I stared in awe as the sun rose above the clouds. Cue all the Psalm praises, worship music, what have you. It was incredible.

Eventually, we landed, got our luggage and visas, and headed out the door. I can't explain it, but as soon as my feet hit the ground in The Land of Transformation, something in me already began to transform. Excitement replaced fear. Energy replaced exhaustion. Calm replaced chaos. I was ecstatic.

We had a six-hour van ride ahead of us, but I didn't mind. What an opportunity to soak in the sights this country has to offer! Most of it was village, but the capital city was bustling and was home to one of the only traffic lights I've seen in my time there. I remember seeing people standing along the road in the villages as we passed by, curious about this bus full of foreigners.

I was struck by the dignity I saw in the people as we passed by. They may not have had much, but they had pride in their possessions. It was on this van ride that I decided I would never take a picture of someone unless I had a relationship with them. Anytime I see pictures in a magazine or newspaper, I wonder if the photographer reimbursed the subject because their presence was providing a service, after all.

At several points in the journey, people stopped the van and offered produce for sale. It was really overwhelming, but the driver took it all in stride and treated us to some snacks throughout the ride. Slowly, our time on the road came to an end, and we were full of anticipation and questions. What was this experience going to be like?

****

Before I left for The Land of Transformation, I met with someone who had gone the year before. I arrived at this place with her words still ringing in my ears: "[Mama] is going to greet you with her entire being."

After 30 hours of travel, we arrived at the hospital looking exhausted and smelling absolutely disgusting. That didn't matter; Mama stepped into the van and greeted all of us with hugs.

As we arrived at the hospital, I was in awe. The hospital grounds were beautiful with a vast array of colorful plant life and lush, green grass. I found out later that couples get married on the grounds! The hospital building structure is one where the walkways are mostly outside with a roof overhead. A lot of the common areas also have a similar setup with the natural outside environment enhancing the inside environment. It was unlike any hospital I had ever seen before. It felt like this hospital was embracing the root of the word *hospital* - hospitality. Although dark times do come to people at this hospital at times, the environment urges its patients and families to hope and to trust that Someone's out there who is in charge of all of it.

The hospital staff was phenomenal. Many staff members were followers of Jesus, and they often sang as they went about their day and weren't afraid to talk about their love for Him. Each morning, there was a time of singing and praying before the work day began, and those times were so powerful. We sang songs I had learned as a child, and singing them in this environment often left me in tears. I think what I was witnessing was true humility, true understanding of our dependence on God. These staff members didn't have all of the material possessions I did, and I think the lack of possessions presented them with a clearer image of who God is and what He means to them.

This hospital is well-known throughout the country. At the time, there were only a handful of neurosurgeons in the entire country, and this hospital employed most of them. It's not unusual for these surgeons to perform seven surgeries a day. Seven BRAIN surgeries. The most common treatment is the insertion of a shunt to drain out the fluid. There is also a second method that these neurosurgeons developed and taught neurosurgeons from the US. This method doesn't involve "foreign objects" in the brain; rather, it reworks some of the pathways in the brain to allow the fluid to drain out naturally. They found this invention necessary because it reduces infection.

Our role for the next two weeks was to love on the mamas and the babies at the hospital and on outreach. I said "mamas" specifically, because in this culture, it is perfectly fine for fathers to leave their families if things become "too difficult." Some fathers did show up, but those instances were rare.

The moms were incredible and so strong. Their strength came from a place of desperation, love, and desire to do anything to make sure their baby was OK. I didn't meet her, but there was one mom who walked the entire way from a neighboring country - a feat only accomplished by a mother's love.

On average, the moms and babies stay for six days at the hospital, so the staff really wants to be intentional about sharing Jesus with them. There is a whole spiritual department, and at that time, Mama was the director. I had just completed a prayer internship, and I had never seen anyone pray like she did. She continually used the name "King of Glory" to refer to God, and though she prayed with authority, there was a simplicity to her prayers, an understanding that she didn't need to impress God with her words. I saw her pray as though she truly believed that the Holy Spirit was inside of her, that they were doing this life together.

****

Over the next two weeks, I began to realize that I did have a story to share. Mama made sure I shared my testimony numerous times, and several women even came to faith in Jesus after listening to me.

During my testimony, I included a segment where I typed on a laptop for them, using only my right hand. Many people have told me that I type faster with one hand than they do with two. Mama took advantage of that skill many times, as she could only hunt and peck. In Mama, I could sense an awe and appreciation of my life and my journey that others up to that point had only taken for granted. To be seen and acknowledged on that level unleashed a sort of healing in me. Just one more reason I call this place *The Land of Transformation*.

Towards the end of the two weeks, my team and I were scheduled to hike at a waterfall. I had experienced several days of sickness, so we thought it best I stay back and hang out with Mama. That day proved to be life-changing.

****

In 2011, Mama started a ministry for the kids who were treated at the hospital for Hydrocephalus and Spina Bifida. She had noticed, over time, that even though the kids were treated at the hospital, certain places in their home cultures were still unwilling to work with them. She felt God nudging her to act, but she was unsure of how to do so. After years of uncertainty, she finally stepped out in faith. In 2012 - just one year later - the dream became reality.

Our team visited the ministry one evening, and the staff was so welcoming and generous! They fed us a meal, and that meal changed my life because it challenged my perspective on generosity. Was I going to go home and tell my people, "We have so much more than they do, yet they gave us all they had!" I've heard that message from teams before, and eventually, that feeling of awe and gratitude wears off in the team. I didn't want this feeling to wear off, though! That meal planted seeds of how I wanted to demonstrate radical generosity in my life.

Our team, the staff and children had a wonderful evening of playing and talking. I remember one boy sitting next to me who would say something in a different language and then lightly hit himself on the head. I asked Mama what he was saying. "I am hitting myself on the head." That made me laugh. I loved watching him laugh, too; while most of the kids had loud, boisterous laughs, this boy laughed soundlessly. The only way to tell that he was laughing was by his shaking body and his bright, dancing eyes. It cracked me up every time.

****

When my team went to the waterfall and I stayed back with Mama and the kids, I wondered what the day would hold for us. She showed me a game that someone gave her and asked me if I knew how to play it. It was Guess Who! At that point, I knew the day would be fun.

Later in the day, Mama said she needed to go to the market and invited me along. As we were making our way through the throngs of people, she asked if I was interested in anything. All throughout the two weeks, I had noticed people wearing sandals made out of tires. I thought that was fascinating, and I wanted a pair. There was a catch, though; due to my physical uniqueness, I can't wear flip-flops. I need sandals with a strap in the back, and my left foot is also slightly smaller than my right foot. Shoe shopping can be a nightmare. We couldn't find a pair anywhere.

Not to be outdone, Mama got an idea. She took me to someone she knew who made tire sandals and explained my situation to him. The next thing I knew, I had a custom-made pair of sandals.

Do you remember when I talked about those friends who entered into my struggle in Chapter 1? The friends who saw my uniqueness as something to be embraced and empowered rather than dismissed and ignored? Mama was one of the very first people to ever enter into my struggle in such a tangible way, and her wholehearted acceptance of my vulnerability opened the door to the friendship of a lifetime.

****

Those two weeks in The Land of Transformation gave me such whiplash. I went from never wanting to go there to never wanting to leave! My life had turned upside down to the point where I decided to do a 3-week fast when I arrived back in the US. At the end of the fast, it became clear to me that I would obtain further education and then return to help with Mama's ministry indefinitely.

Mama and I immediately started to keep in touch, and I found ways to support the ministry. Family and friends grew excited about the vision and helped me with various fundraising goals.

I knew I wanted to go back to The Land of Transformation for another short-term trip, but I didn't know when. One night in the summer of 2013, I heard God say, "Next summer." I didn't know the logistics of it all, but I renewed my passport right away and began to do more dreaming and scheming with Mama.

Four

Land of Transformation

God's promise of "next summer" resulted in a two-month stay in The Land of Transformation in 2014.

I traveled with a team like I did in 2012, but when they left two weeks later, I stayed on. Just one other teammate and I landed when we were supposed to; everyone else missed their connecting flight and didn't arrive until the next day. As the one teammate and I traveled to town, Mama called, and I almost started crying. I was so happy to hear her voice again.

****

The next day was our first day at the hospital. As we entered the chapel for staff devotions, some staff members were deep in silent prayer. I couldn't help myself; I eagerly rushed over, tapped several members on the shoulder, and interrupted them. It was like reuniting with family; I just felt like I was HOME.

Several hours later, Mama pulled me and my teammate into her office. A baby had died. I very quickly learned how naive I was when it came to the logistics of death. When a person dies in the United States, people from the morgue come (I think?), and they take the body away. This description of sorts shows how little I know about the process in my own country. I do know that family members of the deceased do not have to do much with the corpse.

That's not the case in this country, though. I listened numbly as Mama shared that the hospital provides a death certificate, and the mom tucks the body somewhere in her luggage - maybe even her purse - and takes it home with her. To add insult to injury, traveling with a dead body is frowned upon in this country, but there is no other option provided. Adding an element of secrecy to a searing and gut-wrenching experience just seems so cruel. I left that meeting feeling hollow and wondering what the next two months held for me. Thankfully, the rest of our team arrived soon after that, and that provided much-needed distraction.

****

A few days later, I learned that this hospital actually treats adults, too. A woman in her 50s came in with a brain tumor, and the doctors scheduled her for a very invasive surgery. She and her husband spoke English well, and I really connected with the husband. I'll call him Morgan because he reminded me so much of Morgan Freeman - both in looks as well as the way he spoke. He was a believer, and I loved his raw honesty.

Morgan made me laugh as he shared how he came to faith. It was on New Year's Eve, and his sister bugged him to attend church with her. He finally succumbed to her incessant nagging, and he went. The Holy Spirit spoke to him in such a kind and specific way that he decided to give up drinking. He mentioned that he started crying - not because he was overwhelmed by peace or anything - but because he was sad that he now had to give up so much! I found that completely relatable!

On the day of his wife's surgery, I spent multiple hours with Morgan. The surgery was supposed to last six hours, and when I had to leave him, seven hours had already passed. At that point, Morgan had still heard nothing about her progress, and his emotional tank, understandably, was empty. The hours I spent with him reminded me of the beauty and necessity of our emotions. Morgan never gave up on God, and he never made any false declaration about God. At the very same time, he was excruciatingly honest about how helpless he felt and how scared he was. I was honored to be able to sit with him.

Morgan's wife ended up pulling through, and they were able to leave a few days later. I wasn't sure if I would ever see them again, so the hugs and goodbyes were emotional. You get to know someone really well when you walk with them through tough times.

****

One of my favorite weeks of my stay was our team's trip to a village about 8-10 hours away to check on patients of the hospital, so the families wouldn't have to make the arduous journey to the hospital. My team's goal was to show love to the families.

One day, I saw Mama give an extreme dose of tough love. First, she gave a passionate lecture on the importance of finishing malaria medication. She reminded the families that the medication needs to be taken until the last dose, so the body doesn't become immune to the medicine. That led her to reprimand the moms for not coming to the hospital for their children's follow-up appointments. I'll never forget the one thing she said to them, "You may think you don't have the money to come all the way to the hospital, but if you don't come to the hospital, your child may end up dying. Either way, you're going to spend the money." Her translator had a deer-in-the-headlights look: "Do I really have to tell them this?"

There were also many lighthearted moments during this week. As in 2012, I was invited to share my testimony, but that didn't happen until the end of the week. I didn't realize it, but throughout the week I had built up key rapport with the families, simply by trying to speak their language. One common greeting in that language is "Praise the Lord!" and as we got off the bus on our first evening with them, I shouted it enthusiastically! The crowd met the greeting with silence, and then a few seconds later, they erupted in laughter. It wasn't a ridiculing laughter; they were simply amused by me! I imagine the laughter was due to two factors - their surprise that a foreigner would know the phrase and my less-than-perfect pronunciation. As the week went on, I learned more phrases and even started translating for my team in basic situations. It seemed that the more humbly I attempted the language, the more I endeared myself to the families.

When it came time for me to give my testimony, I had everyone's undivided attention. My interactions with the families throughout the week showed them that I was not there to put any semblance of perfection on display. My interactions with the families showed them that I was just as broken as they were, and we were all equally deserving of the love, forgiveness, and wholeness that can be found in Jesus.

I added something new to my testimony that year that I didn't include in 2012. At that point in 2014, I wasn't dating or even desiring to date. Yet I still felt God's nudging to include in my testimony that people with Hydrocephalus and Cerebral Palsy deserve to get married and can get married. I incorporated Romans 4, where Abraham believed in what was to come even though he had no evidence it would actually come to pass. The group found encouragement in that message because one of their greatest fears for their children was that their condition would make them unwanted. I was able to show them, even as a single person, that you can hold both hope for the future as well as gentleness and self-compassion for the present.

****

After two weeks passed, I said goodbye to my teammates and immediately felt how much I was in the minority in my surroundings. It was really important that I experienced that, as it has helped me empathize with people who might be the minority in my area.

I was able to stay in Mama's home for the remaining six weeks, and I was thrilled. We hadn't talked much about meal planning before then, and I brought up the idea of salads. She hadn't ever heard of the concept, and when I explained it to her, she was pleasantly surprised. When people from her country host someone, it is customary to provide for the guest's every need. Salads were the perfect fix because vegetables are cheap, and it's a quick meal. I missed paring knives in those weeks because the only knives Mama had were monstrous. Everyone's reactions to my salads made me laugh so hard. Reactions ranged from head shaking, cringing, to my personal favorite: her son commenting, "Jesus Christ of Nazareth! How can you be satisfied?"

I had some adjusting to do to their food as well. Mama made fish with some sauce on the side, and I didn't put two and two together. I just ate the fish separately, and when I was finished, she said, "You are supposed to eat the fish and the sauce together!" We had a good laugh.

I also tried my hand at food preparation. For example, I cut a chicken's head off, and it was…bloody. Mama's family members have done it often enough so that the chopping is quick and painless. I definitely prolonged the chicken's suffering (and mine) by cutting slowly and painstakingly. It may have helped had I actually been looking and focusing on the task rather than looking away and grimacing the whole time. Whoops!

I wanted to make spaghetti with Mama, too, but my cooking skills aren't the greatest. In the show *Schitt's Creek* [1], there's a scene where mother and son, Moira and David, try to make enchiladas. Neither of them knew what they were doing, so their experience was quite chaotic and unsuccessful. The iconic line from that scene is, "Just fold in the cheese!" My spaghetti experience with Mama had very similar vibes. At one point, Mama's son was helping with the spaghetti, and he seemed to be the only one of us who knew what to do. After some time, he went to do something else, and Mama yelled at him, "Do not go very far!" She and I didn't know when we'd need his help again. I don't remember how the spaghetti turned out, but at least the memory makes me chuckle.

Anything dealing with food in that country requires generosity. If you're eating something and other people are present, the expectation is that you offer some. It's understood in the culture that guests aren't served the bare minimum. When Mama noticed that I was using just a bit of sugar, she always admonished me, "I will not have you economizing my sugar!"

This is a callback to Chapter 3 - radical generosity. One of the ways I try to be generous in my life is that I'd rather put too much food out than too little to offer guests. I'd rather have leftovers than have guests thinking to themselves, "I could have had a little more of that!" Spending eight weeks in The Land of Transformation really challenged me to look at areas in my life where I thought material resources, love, patience, and other good qualities were in short supply. My challenge was to look, instead, at God who "owns the cattle on a thousand hills" (Psalm 50:10) and to trust that in Him, there is an endless supply of everything we need. We do not need to be afraid.

****

Mama was taking an online class at the time and wanted me to be her note-taker. She remembered that I was a fast typist and wanted to benefit from this service, and I was happy to help her! I was a perfectionist in school, and I realized very early on in this process that Mama...wasn't. I wanted us to take our time with the readings, but she kept saying the equivalent of "C equals a degree." She gleefully skimmed over what she found boring and spent more time on what she found interesting. Half of the time, neither of us understood the notes I was typing! As awkward as this experience felt, I admired Mama's desire to simply learn whatever she learned and not to stress about the rest. It was the first time I witnessed someone's joy in learning for learning's sake.

These study sessions either ended our day around 10 pm or started our day around 5 am. I am a morning person, so I love early starts. I need ample time to get ready in the mornings, and if I have to rush around, it's guaranteed to be a rough day. With Mama, it didn't matter when she woke up; she always had to rush. A common question she threw at us in a mildly accusatory tone was, "Where is my PHONE, you people?!" We always looked at her and shook our heads because we were never the reason her phone was missing! I still use that line today when I can't find something.

Mama lived close to the hospital, so we walked there every day. Since it was the rainy season, rain was a daily occurrence, especially around 2 pm. One road we traveled turned into a mud pit, and every day Mama would lament, "How are we going to pass?" One day, she sent me ahead of her with her laptop, and that road was incredibly slick. I concentrated so hard, praying I wouldn't fall and drop the laptop. I also had to pay attention to motorbike drivers, motorbikes being a common form of public transportation. The mud ruts made the motorbikes jostle all over the place, and as one driver bounced past me, he yelled shakily, "This...is...[The Land of Transformation]!" I slipped, slid, and laughed the rest of the way home, thankful to be in that beautiful place. (Side note: when I went back to visit a few years later, that road was PAVED. I was so happy to see that!)

****

Once Mama's course was over, our evenings consisted of relaxing and talking. She was hooked on this super cheesy Spanish soap opera (translated to English, of course). Horrible writing and acting, terrible English voice over, just...wow. But she was dedicated to it, and every night when it was time for it to start, everything else stopped, so she could watch her show. In the beginning, I'd go online or read because I didn't see the point of the show. Gradually, however, I, too, became interested in the show and watched it with her. To the point where we'd talk about the episode after it ended, I'd talk about the characters by name, and she'd tell me I knew more about the show than she did. Um, yikes. Also, when she thought the TV was too quiet, she didn't ask us to "Turn it up," she asked us to "increase the volume."

Evenings also gave us more time to dream about the future of her ministry and how I could be more involved. Mama was sure that God wanted me to take on a fundraising role, and I was...less than sure. Fundraising was never my strong suit, though I did bring up a prophetic message someone had given me one time. It was about having the keys to God's storehouse and telling people, "Oh, you need that? Let me go get that for you!" Mama also shared a sobering confirmation: "I trust that this is God's voice because whenever you promise to send me money, you actually send it." Apparently, Americans had left her high and dry in the past with promises unkept. OK, but still...I'm awful at fundraising!

****

Throughout the two months I spent with her, God continued to reveal Mama's special qualities and to show me what a privilege it could be to embark on this adventure of a lifetime with her. Mama was full of stories in those two months, and I could always tell when it was going to get really good when she said one little word:

Now.

She'd shift positions, pause for dramatic effect, and continue. I have no idea if she did it on purpose, but she did it consistently.

One time, people thought she was practicing witchcraft because there was a giant guarding her garden. In reality, she had been praying that God would protect her plants, and the giant was an angel.

Another time, someone refused to give her a receipt for something for her ministry, and she ended up getting the cops involved..and that was that!

Mama daily encouraged the kids at the ministry to believe miracles could happen to them, and one day the Holy Spirit showed His power and brought physical healing to several students.

James 5:16 isn't lying - the prayer of a righteous person seriously IS powerful and effective! Could God be asking me to get involved this much at the ministry?

****

I spent a lot of time at the hospital in my eight weeks in The Land of Transformation. When I wasn't hanging out with mamas and babies, helping out with administrative duties, or watching a surgery through an outside window, Mama and I could often be found together. I did her computer work for her, we brainstormed about the future, and we spoke to the moms together.

One day, as we wrapped up a speaking session, Mama urgently told me to come to her office. Intrigued by her bursts of energy as always, I followed eagerly.

Mama: God has been talking to me about something, and this meeting just confirmed it! You will be healed! And it will start while you are here.

Me: *sitting in stunned silence*

Let's take a few steps back. Remember that I come from a stoic background. We do our work, we go to church, we don't ruffle feathers...we most definitely don't expect miracles. It's all about God's will, after all. But, *Mama* said this?! Her walk with God was way different than any other person's walk that I had witnessed. Could there be something in this declaration?

Mama: But when you are healed, there will be no evidence that you struggled before. Let's take a video of you trying tasks that you are unable to do, so that when you can do them, you can show others this video as proof.

Me: *sitting in stunned - and now uncomfortably vulnerable - silence* But I don't like to show my imperfections.

After some more encouragement, I agreed to do the video. It was awkward. It was a bit uncomfortable. However, the guys on the camera and equipment crew made it fun, and they kept my dignity intact.

****

The revelations on healing continued a few days later. One evening, Mama and I sat around talking.

Me: I just feel overwhelmed. I don't know how to get my left hand to the skill level of my right hand.

Mama: What do you mean?

Me: Well, aren't both of your hands the same skill level and the same strength?

Mama (emphatically): No, not at all! My left hand is much weaker than my right!

Me: Wait...seriously?

Mama: YES! My left hand does not do the work of my right hand. It supports my right hand.

Me (mind blown): All of these years, I thought my left hand had to be exactly what my right hand was. That's why I shied away from therapy. I felt I had an expectation to fulfill that I physically couldn't. Now that I know my left hand has a role of its own, the idea of therapy is so much more feasible!

These revelations fueled my excitement and belief that God had great things in store for me and for those at the hospital. He was a good God after all...wasn't He?

****

I'm going to close this chapter with the story of Beth and her baby. I met Beth in the ward where the mamas and babies relax and sleep. There is no privacy, so everyone watches everyone else. I typically milled around the ward, trying to strike up conversations and improvise when they didn't speak English. As an introvert, this was the hardest part of my day because it just felt awkward, and I'm not the best improviser. It was different from the outreach because the families at the outreach generally had healthier kids, so the atmosphere was lighter. Here at the hospital, the moms were scared, and the babies weren't playful. It was hard to know what I had to offer.

Then I met Beth.

Her English was perfect, and I thought maybe that was why I was drawn to her. I gravitated to Beth more than to other moms on the ward, and I felt bad because after visiting with other moms, I always headed straight back to Beth.

Her baby was pretty much in constant pain from the buildup of fluid in her brain, due to Hydrocephalus. Staff members would come and tap the fluid several times a day, but it didn't seem to help much. The baby was finally able to go into surgery on her third day at the hospital. By that time, Beth trusted me to the point where she wanted me to stay with her during the surgery.

We didn't hear any updates for 6-7 hours. It was like Morgan and his wife all over again. I watched Beth go through all the emotions, ranging from hope to despair. The baby finally came out of surgery and went to the ICU, which was a normal procedure. The nurses said she was having some breathing issues, but they weren't too concerned. I remember that the news threw Beth for a loop, though. She had trouble focusing on our conversations and was very antsy. I was thankful she agreed to attend a Sunday morning church service for the moms, but right after it was over, she went back to her baby. It broke my heart to see that no distraction was helpful, though I absolutely understood her reality.

The weekend of the church service is when I started understanding why I was so drawn to Beth and her baby. Beth had formed friendships with other moms, and one by one, their children were discharged, so they left. But Beth's baby couldn't leave. I remember her saying at one point that she just wanted to pack up and go home, but deep down, she knew the hospital wouldn't allow it. I was able to be a kind of constant for her.

On Monday, the doctor came up to me and said he thought they knew what the baby's issue was and they planned to have a follow-up surgery the next day. Filled with hope, I went about my day. Later on, Mama found me and said that the baby wasn't doing well. I ran to the ICU and found Beth lying down on a bunk. I asked if it was OK that I was there. She said yes. Within minutes, the doctor came and said that the baby was with Jesus.

Mama soon came and wrapped Beth in a big hug. She prayed and whispered encouragement to Beth and then returned to her "business as usual" face. I remember peppering Mama with questions about what's next, and she essentially told me that this wasn't the hospital's first experience with death, and they knew what to do.

So, now what? Remember when I talked about the Enneagram and said that Fours don't feel their feelings; Fours ARE their feelings? Author Jen Hatmaker says when a person is going through intense grief, the best person to walk with them through it is a Four. I only heard about the Enneagram years after this experience, but Hatmaker's statement makes perfect sense. I didn't know what to DO at the time, but I knew what I was feeling. Everyone else at the hospital had to keep living their life, even though Beth's life had just undergone an excruciating change. My goal for the time being was to be a constant for her, like I had been for the last number of days.

For the next five hours, I had the honor and privilege of sitting with Beth as she began to process the news. It looked like a whole lot of silence on my part. I was living the sentiment "There are no words." There was absolutely nothing I could say to make her feel better or to help her wake up from this nightmare.

The baby died around 2:30 pm, and around 5, Mama told me to try and get Beth to eat something. I had no idea how to do that. How do you urge a bereaved mother to engage in an act of staying alive and nourishing her body, when part of her heart just recently ceased to exist? Thankfully, the nurse manager came and got Beth to eat. She was from the same area as Beth, so she was able to engage her in that language. That seemed to help Beth perk up a bit while she ate.

I remember being so thankful for the nurse manager. She was an older woman who was an absolute rock star in her role, and Beth needed that presence. Beth was only 24, and I was only 27. I didn't have much life wisdom, especially not in parenting! The nurse manager was able to provide a maternal presence that exuded kindness as well as "no nonsense." Beth needed to eat if she wanted to be strong enough for her long journey home. At the same time, the nurse manager spoke with gentleness and tenderness. Beth's English was amazing, but I have to imagine that speaking her native language provided another comfort I couldn't offer her.

After Beth finished eating, I went back beside her, and we held hands and cried. There was one point where she ran out of tears, and I had an abundance of tears! She actually encouraged me at that time! Darkness began to fall, and we didn't even bother to turn on the lights. The darkening room seemed to fit the mood. Soon, I got a call from Mama saying I needed to start heading home. I started frantically thinking of what last-minute things I could do to show my support. I gave Beth the money I had with me, as well as a necklace to help her remember me. I hugged her, said goodbye, and walked out of the room in a daze. It wasn't until a few years later that I wondered why I didn't stay overnight at the hospital until someone picked her up. I just have to trust that she felt carried.

Remember what happens when a baby dies at this hospital? For days afterwards, I thought about Beth having to tuck her baby's body like a package into her luggage and travel with it for twelve hours; she lived clear across the country. Words cannot express the searing pain I felt...and I wasn't even a parent then. That night, I posted on my social media: "For those of you with small children, I ask that you don't yell at them today. Don't stress and vent about the little things. Rejoice in the fact that they are healthy enough to cause mischief. Delight in the simple yet profound truth that they are ALIVE!"

****

It was really hard to head back to the hospital the next day; Mama gave me the OK to stay home if I wanted to. I pushed through with a new sense of awe and appreciation of the staff at the hospital because they deal with these situations regularly and still show up for work the next day. God gave me an incredible gift, though: Morgan, his wife, and her sister were at the hospital for a follow-up appointment! I was so happy to see them and ended up spending most of the day with them.

My trip ended about two weeks later, and the ripple effect that this trip had on my life is still visible today. Remember how I told the group of parents that I believed marriage was possible? Let's talk about guys now!

[1] Levy, Dan, and Eugene Levy. 2016. Review of *Schitt's Creek*Television. Canadian Broadcasting Corporation.

Five

Romance: Stumbling Block or Springboard?

I was boy-crazy from an early age.

In preschool, I had a crush on two boys at the same time. I remember role-playing a lot of *Inspector Gadget*[1] with them, which was really exciting because I wasn't allowed to watch the show at home. I never said anything about my feelings to those boys because who can put feelings into words at 5 years old?

I also had a crush on two different boys in kindergarten - also at the same time. I guess I loved the idea of efficiency back then already! There was a whole group of guys in kindergarten who let me play with their superhero figures and robots. I remember thinking that boys' toys were so much cooler than girls' toys. Who wants to play with dolls when you can make a robot talk?

Looking back, I think I could tell from a young age that being a girl was going to be a lot more complicated than being a boy would be. There seemed to be a lot more complex, two-handed tasks for girls than for boys. I was also so saturated with my own emotion that being around boys was a sort of respite.

I think the crushes stemmed from the fact that...those boys accepted me and welcomed me into their play without question. There was no competition, no sense that identity was threatened. We were equals.

I continued to have crushes throughout elementary and middle school - only one at a time, though! - but my friend group largely became more female. I went from hanging out with boys to talking about them and dreaming about a potential future with some of them.

****

This is a bit of a rabbit trail here, but there is one story from high school that I have to share. It shows my willingness to be spontaneous and my understanding that opportunities may be present one moment and gone the next.

I was a huge fan of Keith Urban, a country singer from Australia. When I was in middle and high school, he was just beginning his career, and if you were a member of his fan club, you could meet him as many times as you wanted. Now there's a lottery system. My parents thought $15 was too much to spend for this experience, so a friend actually purchased a fan club membership for me. I got to meet Urban twice, and in the second meeting, I got the chance of a lifetime. He kissed me on the cheek, and I bravely (stupidly?) asked for a kiss on the lips! He obliged, and I was on Cloud 9 for a long time. It's fascinating that my husband's name is Keith. There must be something in the name!

****

Now that I'm decades out from these memories, my heart aches a bit for younger me. Why did she feel the need to be seen by boys from such a young age? The need to belong is real and valid, but why was a relationship with the opposite gender paramount? Why did it seem to be a status symbol?

I didn't get the encouragement from my parents, that's for sure! I'm pretty sure I told my mom about all of my crushes, and if she didn't laugh in my face, she patted me on the head dismissively and told me to go do something else to get that crazy thought out of my head. It wasn't that she never wanted me to get married. She just knew I was too young to be carrying that responsibility at the time. I think I knew it, too, deep down, but why was that desire so strong?

I know a lot of the blame rests on society. For some reason, we're led to believe we're not complete if we don't have a partner, but even more so...it's "so much more fun" to be a grown-up than it is to be a kid, so let's bypass those years as fast as possible! I remember hearing about relationships in elementary school, already. I'm sure they only lasted a week, but I wondered if I was really missing out on something.

****

As I entered my teen years, I began to learn that there was a Mennonite version of these societal pressures. This version gave me serious whiplash for years. The Mennonite version consisted of two rules:

1. DON'T HAVE SEX.
2. Because of Rule #1, get married as soon as possible.

The first part was loudly stated in youth group. At least once a month, there was a lesson specifically on that topic. There was a popular movement in the US at the time where adults encouraged teens to sign a card pledging their commitment to be a virgin until they got married. I went through this experience at a youth rally, and my parents got me a ring from this movement for my 16th birthday. I wore that ring for years.

The married part was much more subtle. I saw it in the eyes of some people when I asked deep questions about faith. I saw it in people's responses when I talked about going to college after high school. Didn't I know my place? Didn't I know that I was supposed to suffer through high school and declare freedom after graduation?

I need to give a shout-out to my mentor in high school here - you know who you are! You always encouraged my deep questions and my love of learning. You showed me that I can love both God and education. You threw my sanity a lifeline in those years, and I really appreciate you!

The sense I got from Christian circles was that women were discouraged from exploring their talents and interests outside of what's in the home. I didn't date in high school, so I often felt like the odd man out at church. I felt much more welcomed at school, where questions, doubts, and talent exploration were celebrated and embraced. I was given opportunities to try new things and to spread my wings.

I don't want to bash my Christian upbringing because none of what was taught is inherently wrong. It's just that I was different in more ways than one, and the church didn't know what to do with these differences. I was expected to conform to the rest of the group, and when I didn't, I absolutely felt the consequences.

My heart goes out to the version of me in youth group, and I wonder how I can lighten the load of similar girls today.

****

I was so excited to go off to college, even if it was local. I lived just off-campus, and I loved my first taste of independence. It was refreshing to interact with non-Mennonite guys for once; it surprised me that guys could actually be interested in furthering their education. I learned the hard way that going out for coffee with a guy could mean nothing other than a gesture of friendship. Guys were interested in me as a person and wanted to get to know me better as a friend, even if I was hoping for something more. I did find out years later that God was watching out for me in one case, so I guess hindsight really is 20/20.

In the summer after my freshman year, I felt restless about church, so my friend, Jess, invited me to come to hers. She introduced me to the young adult group, and they welcomed me with open arms. Maybe it was because I was older, or maybe it was because of the composition of the group, but all my deep questions were welcomed. Not only did the group encourage my questions, but the participants also wrestled with me, taking my questions deeper than I ever thought possible. I found my people! One attendee of the young adult group was Jess' cousin, Keith. Little did I realize how important he would become to me eight years later.

****

People always told me that if I stopped thinking about guys, maybe a relationship would happen then. I needed to "let go" in a sense to show God that I was ready for a relationship.

That logic frustrated me. Why did I have to prove that I was ready for something? It seems that "not being ready" for something is shameful; if we're not ready, then there is something wrong with us.

When I became a parent, it hit me - no one gives birth to full-sized adults. (Can I get a hallelujah?!) We give birth to tiny, helpless beings who do nothing to contribute to the world around them. They're not ready for anything! Yet we love them and provide for their every need relating to comfort, clothing, cleanliness, and more. We know that, in time, and as their development allows, they will meet every milestone and accomplish every task they were meant to.

It's not about the destination: the relationship, the job, the house; that's only part of it. It's about looking around us as we journey and about taking advantage of the opportunities along our path. Maybe the opportunities will help us when we reach our destination, or maybe their role is to strengthen us and cultivate perseverance.

I remember a friend sharing a vision God gave her. She was running on a high school track, around and around, lap after lap. God told her that even though she thinks nothing is happening in the mundane training, she should look at her legs. There she would see the strengthening and the muscle build up. I have thought about that vision often.

I just want to say it again – No matter the situation, if you're not ready, there's nothing wrong with you.

****

Forgetting about guys was a slow process. In 2013, I had an idea to start a journey of noticing how God pursues me. I decided to embark on a 100-day challenge and come away each day with at least one example of how God met me. I armed myself with the knowledge found in Psalm 23, stating, "Surely goodness and mercy will follow me," which is actually, "chase and pursue." How cool is that?

Over those 100 days, I actually did forget about guys. I fell deeper in love with something else I mentioned before - The Land of Transformation - with its breathtaking views and some of the best people on the planet. Those 100 days gave me sharper vision and clearer focus on what my final destination should be. After getting further education, I planned on moving there permanently.

But God....

****

A year prior to the 100-day challenge, I participated in a prayer internship through a local house of prayer. Many people looked at me quizzically, "You're going to pay to pray?" It was a lot more than that and life-changing in more than one way. I knew by that point that Keith was a prayer warrior, so I told him to join the internship that year. He declined. He ended up participating in the internship in the spring of 2014 instead. The spring of 2014 found me up to my neck in full-time graduate course work, two part-time jobs, and preparation to spend July and August in The Land of Transformation. My face was set like flint towards my goals, and I was oblivious to anything else.

Sometime in June, I got a message from Keith asking if we could have lunch together. The invitation came out of nowhere. I called my close friend Jess (his cousin) and asked if she had any idea why he suggested this. She was just as much in the dark. I agreed with some hesitation, and we set a date for about a week later at a restaurant.

Leading up to the meeting, I was wondering what to do if we happened to see people we knew. What would we say? They'd definitely be talking about us after we left as one does in my area. And of course, it happened! The acquaintances were gracious and kept their questions to themselves, and we found a table. Keith wanted to meet with me to discuss life after the internship. The internship creates a tight-knit community, but after the internship ends, it leaves the participant a bit out of sorts. Several months later, Keith's internship group got together, and he said that the sense of community was gone even after such a short time. Community is hard to navigate, and it needs a lot of intentional TLC!

I understood where he was coming from, but the whole time, I was thinking, "Why is he meeting with me? Why isn't he processing with someone from his own group?"

After that meeting, I promptly forgot about him and resumed my chaotic life. The time to head to the Land of Transformation would happen soon, and I wanted to be completely present for it.

****

A few months later, I returned to the US more fully determined than ever that at some point, I was going to move to this land that I loved and stay indefinitely. Nothing could change my mind.

Shortly after I came home, Keith asked if we could meet up because he wanted to hear more about the trip. I agreed and told myself this was the last meeting. A few weeks later, I held an event at my church to talk about my time, and I saw him in the audience. I made sure to clearly state that I wasn't done with the Land of Transformation. Nothing was going to deter me, and I needed Keith to realize that. Little did I realize that my stubbornness had met its match.

****

Later that week, Keith texted me and asked if I would like to go to the fair with him, and I wanted to throw my phone against a wall at work. Why is he still reaching out?! With much agitation, I said yes.

I was living with my parents at the time, and up to that point, they knew nothing of this guy. I didn't want to go home after work to change, because I wanted to avoid any and all interrogation about plans for the evening. I decided to meet him in my "attractive" work attire at the local house of prayer where he was singing that night and waited until he was finished.

We drove to the fair together, and I think we were mostly silent. My mind was screaming the whole time, "What is going on here?! If he doesn't explain himself by the end of tonight, you need to initiate the conversation and get to the bottom of this!"

We walked around the fair, and thankfully, conversation flowed more easily then. At one point, he asked if I was hungry, and I said, "No, I didn't bring any money along for anything, so I'm fine." He said, "I'm hungry for monkey bread, so let's share some!" That was intriguing...on our other two dates (?), we each paid our own way and ate our own food. Anxiously, I waited as he purchased the monkey bread, and we found a table. At this point, I was eating without tasting, and listening to him talk without understanding, because my mind was screaming at me to say something.

Eventually, he spoke up. He said it was great hanging out with me as a friend but wondered if I'd be interested in taking the relationship deeper. Welp, there it was, folks! That was his actual intention; for once, I wasn't reading into things!

****

Remember when I said I had actually forgotten about guys? This forgetfulness resulted in me getting shocked to my core at his question, as though I had fallen through thin ice, and I needed to recover. I asked if we could take a month to pray about it because I needed time to desire a relationship again! He met two of my three non-negotiables: He loved Jesus, and he wasn't afraid to delve into deep conversation topics. The third important point in my checklist was my hang-up: he didn't want to travel. I always imagined my husband and I would be globetrotters. We agreed to talk off and on throughout the month but would just wait until the end of the month to become official if it came to that.

I got home around 10:30 that night and emailed Mama right away. What was she going to say? Was she going to feel betrayed? We made all these plans, and now what? She wrote back the next day, absolutely thrilled with the news. Her mantra to me then, as it was a few months before, was: "Have your peace, my sister." She believed if God wanted this relationship to happen, then everything would fall into place.

A few days later, I won tickets to a Christian concert later that week – my first time ever calling in and actually winning! I was hesitant about asking Keith to join me, but I did. The concert was a few days away, and I really felt plagued by doubts. I wasn't exactly "damaged goods," but I was broken. Marriage already confronts couples with "in sickness and in health," so why would he want to enter into a lifelong relationship with a condition that's already present?

On the way to the show, Keith opened up out of nowhere. "So, when the Holy Spirit brought your name to mind to pursue a relationship with, I wrestled with Him. I didn't know what to do about your disability. Then God got stern with me. 'This isn't her fault. This is an attitude you need to work through.' So, I am willing to enter into this journey with you."

Well, I was stunned. I hadn't even mentioned the few days of dark thoughts I had, and God gave me this?! We had a great time at the concert, and I didn't sleep much that night. The next day, I called him and asked if we could make it official then and there. After his vulnerability the previous night, I had no doubts about the relationship anymore. He chuckled and said, "You wanted to wait a month, so let's wait a month!"

Throughout the month, we had several times of connection and found we agreed on a lot of lifestyle choices. Starting a relationship seemed logical, so on October 26, 2014, over lots of laughter, the *Sonic the* Hedgehog[2] video game, and snacks, we officially became a couple.

NOTES

[1] Bianchi, Bruno. 1985. "Inspector Gadget." Television.
[2] Sonic Team. *Sonic Mega Collection Plus.* PS2, 2004. USA.

Six

From Dating to I Do

Remember that 100-day challenge I went on to see how God was pursuing me? When Keith and I started dating, I asked him when he started thinking about me. He said it was February of 2014. After some quick calculations, I realized...that's when my challenge ended! I went through that challenge with no expectations, and I think that's when God does His best work!

It was fun telling friends and family we were a couple. Most people had the same reaction - a brief look of surprise/confusion, followed by excitement, "Ohhhh, I see it now! That actually makes perfect sense!" I understand their confusion; I never would have put us together, and the Holy Spirit had to tap Keith on the shoulder twice to get his full cooperation. There was one couple at our church who was actually not surprised. They had been thinking all along we'd be a great pair, and one Sunday they whispered to each other, "Keith and Michelle are sitting BESIDE each other!"

We quickly realized that our relationship was going to fall under the typical "emotional woman, rational man" category. I freaked out a lot, and he listened...a lot. He and I talked about how men have mental boxes for things, while women's thoughts were like spaghetti, all intertwined and messy. However, when I made that phone call to him after the concert, it turned out his patience was just a front. He said his boxes were actually all flipped over, with all sense of order lost. He said he didn't get much work done that day!

As with anything in life, beginnings can be clunky. This was my first relationship and Keith's second. We're both relatively serious people, so at least for me, laughing with him was awkward at first. I always thought, "Wait, are we doing this dating thing right?" Or, "Is he laughing at me in some sense?" It's the struggle of the classic over-thinker.

I'm a Highly Sensitive Person, so I grew up constantly hearing, "I was just kidding!" "Stop being so sensitive!" Of course, I loved to laugh, but I learned to question the motives behind other people's laughter - and my own. Can laughter truly be pure? Or is there usually a catch, a slight insult behind it? I often mistrusted laughter.

But here is one of the gifts God has given me in Keith that I never knew I needed. Keith does not do sarcasm. He understands it, of course, but he does not see a purpose for it! We were watching a movie one time, and he actually paused it to wonder why they needed sarcasm in that particular scene. What was the point?

I cannot express how HEALING this has been for me. To know that he is never going to laugh AT me, but that we are free to laugh at situations TOGETHER! On the same team! It has been so FREE-ING.

****

With Keith, still waters run deep. He doesn't feel the need to fill up space with small talk. We went to the Farm Show one time, and on the bus ride back to our car, some guy turned to us and jokingly asked, "Would you guys be quiet already?" Keith said to me after the fact, "Some people just aren't comfortable with introverts." I hadn't thought of it like that before, but it made sense. As I saw on social media one time, the world urges introverts to speak up, but no one encourages extroverts to shut up.

His comfort level with quiet quickly caught on to me. To be able to go to his place, flop on the couch after a long day and not feel pressure to say anything? It was magical.

Not only is he quiet in speech but also on foot! He is a ninja, plain and simple. Since being married to him, I have thrown laundry, screamed, and almost walked into him in the dark. One night around midnight, I was in the bathroom, doing my thing and trying to stay sleepy. Out of nowhere, Keith came in and asked, "Is everything OK?!" (For some reason, when I got out of bed, he thought I was running. I wasn't).

I jumped out of my skin. So much for trying to stay asleep! He actually had to come over and calm me down because I was shaking! He admitted, "Yeah, I'm still learning about you..." I felt bad that was my reaction, but I CAN'T HELP IT. Gotta love God's humor - pairing a ninja with a jumpy person!

****

Keith is the type of guy who does what needs to be done, no questions asked. On one of our first dates, I wanted to make him a meal. Even though I wanted to do it on my own, he saw where I could use help and jumped right in. His willingness to help sometimes brings him to new creative heights. Because of my Cerebral Palsy, my left hand moves a lot - of its own free will - and it makes hand holding interesting. The first time we realized this little quirk, he simply intertwined our fingers, so my hand couldn't go anywhere. I'm so thankful for his quick thinking and for his embrace of all that could be awkward.

Early on in our relationship, though, I put that quality to the test. I came down with pink eye over the weekend. The only treatment for this is drops, and of course, my parents were away. Who was I going to get to help me? Keith wouldn't want to do this for me so early in our relationship! Surely, he'd see how tedious life with me would be and break it off. Turns out, I was way wrong about his character. He very willingly jumped in and helped, and I was blessed so much by his kindness.

****

In early 2015, I had the pleasure of hosting Mama on her first trip to the US! Keith went with me to pick her up, and it was such a joyous reunion. The drive back home was about a half hour, and Mama was full of questions for Keith - curious questions, not interrogative. After he dropped us off, Mama said, "I like him. A lot!"

It was just Mama and me at home that night, and we picked up right where we left off. After she filled me in on all of the local gossip, she displayed her vulnerability. Her time in the US showed her that marriage can look a lot different from what she was used to. At the time, she was in a marriage that was essentially "marriage in name only." In fact, her "husband" lived somewhere else with another woman and was a respected elder in a church! She talked about divorce and how women couldn't initiate it in her country.

Mama recounted an experience that lasted for years where her "husband" spread rumors about her, and a lot of people, including her own children, believed the lies. I found it astounding that she never fought back but took it all to Jesus in prayer. She knew He was her ultimate defender, and she resigned herself to take whatever verbal abuse might come her way from community members. Eventually, her children all came to her in tears, asking her to forgive them for believing the lies about her. Those years were incredibly hard, so the sweet emotional homecoming of her children was such an incredible victory. This victory resulted in rock-solid conviction that she was worth a lot more than she was receiving, and she was determined to find that worth in her relationship with Jesus.

Mama continued with that posture of prayer in her "marriage," but she shared that if she ever remarried, she'd want it to be to someone from a different country. She actually talked to me about men she felt attracted to. I was honored she'd want to share all of this...and extremely grateful for the budding relationship Keith and I had.

We had such an amazing four days together. One evening, she spoke about her children's ministry at my church. We also had some hilarious experiences in restaurants, and she even told my sister that she'd "be back next year for the wedding of these two!" That's Mama - always speaking her mind!

One spontaneous activity that neither of us was expecting was a root canal for her! Before she visited me, I was at the dentist, and I heard the Holy Spirit clearly say, "Make an appointment for Mama." So I did!

Mama told me later how relaxed she felt in the dentist's chair, "It was like they healed you even before they started working!" she exclaimed. Her teeth were healthy, just one cavity and one tooth that could either be extracted or saved with a root canal. I had to do some quick thinking. I definitely wanted to get the cavity filled for her, but root canals are expensive! The dentist briefly explained the root canal procedure, and I asked Mama what she thought, especially since steps in the procedure might possibly go wrong. She said, "Are you sure?" I said, 'Yes!" Without knowing where exactly all the money would come from for this procedure, I accepted the cost in a leap of faith.

Throughout this process, Keith got a front row seat to my desire that everyone gets everything they need...and then some. He contributed some money towards the root canal, and thank God, the doctor did the procedure at half price! I fundraised for the rest, and the money came in. I know it meant a lot to Mama, and I think Keith was touched, too.

****

After saying a hard goodbye to Mama, I turned my attention back to my dating relationship, and in June of 2015, Keith asked if we could go to the mall. Wait...we never went to the mall. The stereotypical roles of couples and shopping were switched in our situation. I loathe shopping. My goal is to get in, get what I need, and get out. Keith enjoys browsing and bargain hunting. I wasn't along for this experience, but one time at the mall, he saw a shirt that he liked, took a picture, and went to see if he could find it cheaper at another store! I always say, you either spend time or money in life, and within reason, I typically choose money!

I agreed to the suggestion but was curious about his intention. On the way to the mall, I felt like a ton of bricks hit me - he wanted to take me ring shopping! In true Keith fashion, though, we browsed clothing stores, shoe stores, got a snack, and then..."Oh hey, let's go to this jewelry store!" Bingo!

The whole experience felt surreal, and it didn't take long until I decided on one with three small diamonds. I liked the symbol of the Trinity being on prominent display in our marriage. He didn't buy the ring there, but my choice gave him an idea of what to look for. Now the clock was ticking. When would he pop the question?

****

About five weeks later, we were going to meet some friends for lunch at a park. We were running late thanks to Keith (a faint foreshadowing of what was to come in life!), and I was getting frustrated. He said he forgot one last thing and ran upstairs. I wasn't happy. The couple we were meeting had kids, and I wondered how they were holding up without food.

Eventually, we made it to the park, and we had a wonderful lunch and conversation. I took more time than usual to say goodbye to the family because I don't see them often. When I turned back to Keith, he was down on one knee, holding the ring box in his hand!

My first thought was, "Is he serious?! Not now!" I was so lost in thought that he had to say my name several times to get my attention. But it happened! I could still see my friends in the distance, so I shouted their names but with no luck. After I posted about the proposal on social media, my friends from that lunch were very curious about when exactly he proposed. They were really surprised to hear they were still in the parking lot and just missed the moment by a minute or so.

Though the proposal was short and sweet, the thought behind it wasn't. Keith wanted to make sure he proposed in our 8th month of dating because eight is the number of new beginnings. I loved that attention to detail.

****

I remember constantly looking at my engagement ring; I'd maneuver it in any way I could to blind myself in the reflection. I worked at a children's summer program, and two days after Keith proposed, I went with the program to a cave. I decided I'd leave the ring behind because I did not want to look all over a creepy cave in the event of it slipping off!

Because I was still getting my Master's Degree, we decided on a year-long engagement. One pastor friend of ours said, "Man, that is a long time to wait! If you ever get too impatient, just come to my office, and we'll get the job done!" I chuckled and was thankful that we had so many people in our corner.

Remember when I mentioned my dislike of shopping a few pages ago? That dislike also applied to wedding traditions. Most women love wedding dress shopping, but I was dreading it. I decided to keep it simple and go to only one shop. I knew I'd like something at every place I browsed, so why drag it out? I went with my mom, my sister and my nieces to a local shop. I had heard horror stories about chain wedding stores, so I wanted to keep the process simple and close by. I love the honesty of kids. As I walked out in a super heavy and clunky dress, my oldest niece declared, "I don't like that one!" I didn't, either!

The bridal shop owner said she always watches the bride's eyes as she brings out the dresses to try on. After several traditional dress vetoes, she said, "Let's try something different." She brought out a bridesmaid's dress, and she said my eyes lit up! I loved it; it screamed simplicity. It was a leap of faith, though...she only had it in red, and I'd only see it in white once the dress fitting rolled around. (It was perfect!) I was in and out of the store in about an hour.

****

Of course, Mama was thrilled for us, and in addition to bringing her over for the wedding, we began to plan for a US-wide tour for her to share information about her ministry. Over her years of working at the hospital, she met many Americans who jumped at the chance to host her.

I told her she was going to be the guest of honor at the wedding, and she asked me what that meant. I had no idea since I just made it up on the spot, but it ended up meaning that Keith walked her down the aisle after he walked our moms down.

****

Since we were planning to get married in the summer, we tossed around the idea of having the wedding outdoors. It's true that I'm a planner, but I'm also an efficient planner, so the less we had to plan, the better. I didn't feel like having a plan B in case it rained, so we tossed the idea aside.

Thank goodness we planned everything indoors; rain was the backdrop of the day. Surprisingly, I ended up welcoming the rain. The rain actually ushered in a calm atmosphere. All of the girls in my bridal party are calm by nature, and as we were getting our hair done, the stylists said this was the most relaxed bridal atmosphere they'd ever experienced! Mama was back with us as we were getting our hair done and even fell asleep! I was so thankful for the way the day started.

The relaxed nature of the day began to wane, however, a few hours later. I mentioned earlier that Keith tends to run fashionably late. Our wedding day ended up being no different; the photographers arrived before he did! I tried to hold it together but did a miserable job of it. All of my insecurities started surfacing; it's the first day of the rest of our lives together, and he was running late?!

We had decided to do "first look" pictures, and that was the game changer. Finally seeing Keith and having him hold me was the grounding that I needed. We decided to take all the outdoor pictures under the carport at the church, and the rain provided a soothing and healing backdrop.

****

All of a sudden, it was time! A year of planning led to this moment. As I stood at the top of the aisle, I felt intimidated. It's not every day that people stand when I enter a room. I felt a bit vulnerable because I normally wear glasses - never contacts - and on this day, I didn't want the glasses' glare to interfere with any pictures, so my vision was blurry as I began to walk down the aisle. I also felt a bit dazed as my dad walked me down the aisle, and the daze held as we approached the front of the church. What was I supposed to do next?! People say girls tend to marry someone like their dad, and in that moment, I could see it. Gently, patiently, and wordlessly, my dad nudged me over to Keith. Ohhhh, that's right, I'm getting married today!

After we walked up the aisle as a married couple, Keith immediately whisked me to the elevator to go upstairs. I loved his spontaneity; he wanted a few minutes alone with me before more chaos ensued. We spent about five minutes simply reveling in the fact that we were officially husband and wife.

We had plans to take some outdoor pictures at a nearby pond, but the rain stopped all of that. Some people may have found that frustrating, but I actually found it liberating. The rain forced us to slow down and intentionally spend time with the people we love. Keith now had enough time to write down how the emcee would introduce his groomsmen. I also heard about our emcee crying throughout the whole ceremony. Mama was chatting with her host for the next leg of her trip, so I was glad she was occupied. Keith and I had time to take everything in.

None of our bridal party felt up to sharing at the reception, so we asked Mama to speak and to say a blessing. It was beautiful and heartfelt.

Having run on adrenaline all day, I remember the exact moment I crashed. My eyes felt heavy, my arms and legs felt like they had a weight on them, and I didn't know how to socialize anymore. Thankfully, Keith was ready to go.

Here we go, God! We're ready for what You have in store for us! Or...were we?

Seven

Kids Change Everything

Leading up to our wedding, we had this conversation with Mama:

Mama: When do the two of you intend to have children?
Keith and I: Uhhhhh, not sure yet.
Mama: How many do you intend to have?
Michelle: Three?
Mama: If money were not an issue, how many children would you want to have?
Keith: Five!
Michelle: ExCUSE me?!

When Mama was giving the blessing at our reception, the photographer got a picture of our expressions the exact minute she said, "I will be back in the US sometime to help carry babies!" We just shook our heads, not at all surprised that Mama would make such a bold statement of faith.

****

Growing up, I said I wanted kids, but it was always a theoretical statement because I never made an effort to learn how to work with young kids. For one thing, I never babysat; I'm not sure if people just didn't ask or if they were worried that my physical uniqueness might be an issue.

In my 8th-grade Family and Consumer Science class, there was a unit on children. I took a lifelike baby doll home and had to turn a key whenever it cried. It cried a lot. As it turns out, I was turning the key wrong! I wish I had been as bold as a classmate of mine who ended up putting his doll out in the car overnight! At least he had the excuse of accidentally being given a demonstration doll that wasn't meant for students. I was just clumsy!

At the end of that children's unit, we were invited to bring a young child with us to class for some preschool activities. I didn't really know many young kids, so I brought my sister's boyfriend's niece. That title alone implies it was all a stretch, and I should have simply avoided the awkward encounter. Her mom dropped her off and went to wait in the lobby until the end of class. The girl wasn't having it - understandably - and raced out of the room, sobbing. Everyone just stared at me, so I ran out of the room after her, yelling for her to slow down and wait for me.

My friend, who was in art class at the time, just a few doors down from my class, told me that as I ran past, all activity in her room stopped. I don't remember how the ordeal all ended; I think her mom joined us in the class, and the rest of the period passed uneventfully.

****

My discomfort and awkwardness around children continued throughout high school and college. Whenever I could, I made it abundantly clear that I was going to work with high school kids because they just made more sense to me.

Years before my current role as a high school German teacher, I was involved with a youth ministry, and I loved sitting at students' feet and listening to their stories. I discovered my ability to keep a conversation going by asking questions, and as long as the student was talkative, conversations could last an hour or more. I learned the fascinating paradox that the more I listened and validated the students, the more interesting they thought I was! That doesn't make sense, but a lot of the beautiful things in life don't make sense. The more we give of ourselves, the more we receive.

****

Before I went to the Land of Transformation for the first time, I felt the Holy Spirit say, "Something that's dormant inside of you is going to become visible." I didn't realize it until after I came home, but it had to do with younger children! Before the trip, if I smiled at a baby or a young child, they just stared at me, especially if I didn't know them. After coming home, though, it all changed! Babies beamed or giggled; young children smiled shyly. I still don't know what changed. Was it a certain level of confidence? Was it a change of heart that I had something to offer them, and they had something to offer me? Whatever it was, it left me feeling cautiously excited; where would this new feeling (ability, perhaps?) take me?

I started volunteering at a preschool for kids with disabilities in early 2013 - the same preschool I had attended as a toddler - and I was pleasantly surprised by my interactions with the kids. They appreciated me; they wanted to be with me! I have one memory of a trip to a park. I was always a little nervous when we were that "hands-on" with the kids, because my physical uniqueness became more apparent. I was walking around with the cutest little boy ever, and the experience was a bit awkward but totally successful. One of our therapists came over to work with him, and he resisted! He kept reaching for me! The knowledge that he was perfectly happy hanging out with me, even though I felt clumsy, was truly a gift. It was one of the first times I realized that when children feel safe and secure, they can be content anywhere.

Volunteering at the preschool eventually turned into a job, and I worked there for about two years. I learned so much in those two years and am grateful for the opportunity. I even brought Mama to visit so she could see what opportunities were possible for children in her country. I loved seeing my two worlds come together on that day.

****

Remember when I had those few days of doubt before Keith and I became official? A huge reason for those doubts was that I didn't know if I could physically care for children. Loving a child is one thing; I never doubted that I would have love for my kids; however, could I physically care for a baby when my own fine-motor skills were those of a young child?

I think a lot about the different times when Keith stepped into my physical uniqueness while keeping my dignity intact. Those instances showed me that I wouldn't have to do motherhood alone, that he would be with me every step of the way. He reminded me that life didn't have to be perfect; messiness was more fun, anyway.

****

In Chapter 6, I shared that Keith got the idea to intertwine our fingers while holding hands, so my left hand wouldn't go anywhere. The mental picture of our fingers intertwined makes me realize the hidden strengths that have come along with my physical uniqueness. These hidden strengths are what opened my eyes to the fact that I could actually be a mother someday.

My first hidden strength is that I can't multitask. Studies show that no one can truly multitask; I'm just honest enough to admit I can't! Seriously, though, I can't do more than one thing at a time. When it's raining, I'm just used to getting wet because I can't free up my strong hand with something as "frivolous" as an umbrella. I would love to hold a mug of hot chocolate while reading a book, but that's not possible. I am forced to do one thing at a time, and it has kept my to-do list humble because my limitations are always right in front of me.

Just a side note, if you've ever said to me, "Man, I wish I had more than two hands!" I would always inwardly chuckle when I saw the instant regret on your face after you said it! There are no hard feelings, and I know we'd all be saying this even if we had four hands. On a positive note, having one main hand to get through life has shown me how to prioritize, and I don't know if I would have learned the skill so quickly had I had two capable hands.

In this chapter's opening conversation, I said I wanted three kids because it was what I was used to. Keith and I each come from a family with three kids, and I knew a lot of other families with three kids. As we started our marriage, however, I gradually felt the Holy Spirit urging me to change my thinking. He invited me to think, "I will be grateful for whoever and however many come our way. If there won't be any, well, we'll cross that bridge when we get there."

The way I reframed my thoughts about how many kids we'd have lines up with my acceptance of only doing one task at a time. Those doubts that I had early on in our relationship did have grains of truth to them, after all. Parenthood was going to be a different experience for me than for other people, and I couldn't ignore that. If I had multiple young kids running around me with my limited ability to do more than one thing at a time, that's a recipe for disaster.

****

I don't know if I'd call it a movement, but there is a trend in my area to have bigger families. Couples in my area take God's command in Genesis to be fruitful and multiply very seriously. There is nothing wrong with big families, and there is a lot of love in those families that I know. I just have to wonder what's truly driving the creation of big families. If a family has honestly evaluated their situation and finds the thought of a big family exciting and adventurous and feels confident they can be successful, that's one thing. However, I've heard in some cases, "God *called us* to have just one more child" or "God *has told us* we were going to have x number of children." This might sound heretical, but...

What if God puts the size of our family into our own hands? Of course, He has a plan and endless love for each child who comes along, but what if He invites us to look at our unique situation and to decide whether or not we have more? What if He doesn't want to be **the** reason we have more kids?

This brings me to the next hidden strength my physical uniqueness gives me - the empathy and ability to look at children as unique individuals, not as an extension of some family expectations. As I've learned often enough in my own life, I've fallen short of many (un)spoken expectations due to my physical uniqueness, so I know what it feels like to disappoint others. I didn't want to burden any future children with arbitrary hoops to jump through to gain my love and affection.

As Keith and I began talking about starting a family, I started following pages on social media that encouraged me to treat my future children as individuals. The posts ranged from sitting with children through meltdowns to food struggles and sleep issues. It was all eye-opening to me and Keith. We certainly weren't raised with these insights. In fact, a lot of families in our area tend to follow certain Christian literature that frowns on everything we were learning from these social media pages.

That's when it hit me. That very literature is what allows people to have so many children. If the #1 goal of parenting is to teach your children that obedience is paramount, then having 5+ children is easy; you just mold the next kid to be the same as the others before it. I was so thankful that Keith was willing to buck the trend of what we knew as traditional parenting. We didn't know what our parenting style was going to look like, but we knew we were united, and that was enough for us.

In Chapter 2, I mentioned 1 Corinthians 13 and how the chapter only provides instructions for the giver of love; it says nothing about the one who receives the love. If I had to choose one Scripture I've been muddling through since becoming a parent, it's this one. I remember one time being so frustrated, and God gently reminded me, "Love is patient, you know." Wait, so it's not 'Love demands obedience' or 'Love focuses on outward behavior?"

Nope, it's none of that. Patience isn't concerned with the outcome. It's focused on the present. Not any progress taking place in the present, just the present moment. Patience trusts that the outcome is in better hands than ours and holds fast to the promise that the cared-for are the carefree.

Because love is patient, it invites situations where patience is required. Because love is kind, it puts itself in situations where kindness is the solution. Because love does not envy, it lays itself down in situations where surrender is the only answer.

But I'm getting ahead of myself here.

****

I remember when we started trying to conceive. We told a few people that we were trying, and of course, Mama had to throw her two cents in: "Are you aware that there are certain days when it is easier to get pregnant? Are you trying on those days?" YES, Mama!

I went back to the neurologist I hadn't seen since 2012 just to cover all my bases. I remember talking to the tech, and he said, "Oh, a friend of mine has Hydrocephalus. He was never concerned about pregnancy..." he trailed off as the awkwardness of what he was saying caught up with him. I still chuckle when I think about that memory.

I also went to my primary doctor to learn all that I could before this journey started. A lot of doctors in this practice are Christians, and the atmosphere is truly one of peace and healing. She prayed with me, and I remember her handling a delicate subject in the kindest way possible: "Michelle, if you miscarry, there is nothing you can do to stop it, and there is nothing you did to cause it." I wonder how many women have needed to be reminded of that. I was grateful for that encouragement to be gentle with myself, no matter what our journey held.

****

We started trying in the fall of 2018, and that fall found me starting my 4th year as a part-time German teacher, a position I loved and was content with. I took advantage of free afternoons to check things off my to-do list and sometimes even to socialize. I also liked the idea of working part-time as a mom because I could still spend a lot of the day with my child.

A year prior, I had wrapped up my Master's Degree journey in Special Education, and I breathed so deeply. It was such a relief not to have any extra coursework, and I actually felt something I hadn't felt in a while - a sense of boredom! That sense of boredom was another indication that now might be a good time to start a family.

In November 2018, the Director of Special Education at my school reached out and offered me a part-time position in Special Education, turning my status into full-time. I wouldn't have to interview or anything; the position was mine if I wanted it! Whoa. Keith and I didn't need to talk too much about it; the extra money would be nice, and let's be honest - what if we weren't going to be parents? We wanted to take the best course of action with the information we had right in front of us. Here's what was right in front of us - a job offer that I didn't interview for that would improve our financial status and two months of no pregnancy.

****

Here's the third hidden strength that my physical uniqueness has given me - a sense of surrender. Do not get me wrong; I have plenty of areas where I am holding onto things with a death grip, but those are topics for another book. Being a parent is an area where I have typically had the attitude of "If it happens, it happens." I do remember a friend getting pregnant before me, and as she was talking to someone excitedly one night, I felt a twinge of sadness that it hadn't happened for me yet. Generally, though, I have had open hands towards the topic of motherhood.

So, with hands open to whatever the future held, I accepted the job offer. I started at the beginning of December. Two weeks later, I found out I was pregnant, and life was about to get so much more chaotic!

****

I'm so thankful that, if it weren't for all the appointments in the second half of my pregnancy, I'd hardly have noticed I was pregnant. I felt great and at peace about everything. Because of my physical uniqueness, my pregnancy was considered high-risk, so I had more appointments than the average pregnancy requires. I was OK with that because I got a lot more ultrasound pictures than I was expecting.

I had so much respect for the ultrasound techs; I had to wonder if they were really good at those *Magic Eye*[1] books. "Oh, baby's folded in half with their feet over their head." How do they even know what they're looking at?! There's an episode of *Friends*[2] where Ross and Rachel saw the first ultrasound of their baby, and Rachel cried. Not because she was so excited to see her baby, though. She was crying because even with the tech's help, she couldn't see the baby anywhere! I was Rachel during the ultrasounds; I didn't cry, though; I just smiled and nodded. The techs' talents blew my mind every time.

****

At the 20-week ultrasound, the tech looked at the brain first and uttered these words: "Everything's perfect." For someone who has literally gone through brain surgery for hydrocephalus, hearing those words ran deep. Thank You, Jesus! The doctor did think the baby's growth wasn't matching up with the number of weeks of the pregnancy, so that added even more appointments to the calendar. I was determined to focus on the silver lining of getting to see my baby more often than expected.

When I entered my third trimester, I had to start non-stress tests once a week that monitored my baby's heart rate for 20-40 minutes. They really should call them stress tests, because I sat there low-key stressing the whole time.

I have two specific memories from these tests. The tests either took place in an actual labor and delivery room or in a big room with beds separated by curtains. In those particular rooms, privacy was nonexistent. I remember sitting there while the nurse was talking with the patient on the other side of the curtain. I was trying not to eavesdrop, but I was pretty sure I heard the nurse ask, "Are you still on meth?" The patient replied, "Yeah, I would go crazy without it." Right away, I went into judgment mode. 'I am trying my hardest to do the right thing, and I'm in this situation. You're not even trying!' After a few minutes, I felt the Holy Spirit say, "OK, you need to check yourself here. You don't know her story, and you don't know where you'd end up if you were in her shoes!' Oof, another reminder that I am privileged and that given a perfect storm of challenges, I might have turned out like she did.

One day, the 'non-stress' portion of the test turned into 'STRESS'. At one point, they saw that I had a contraction that dropped the baby's heart rate super low. They scheduled me for an ultrasound and gave me a steroid shot to strengthen the baby's lungs - in the event that I'd have to DELIVER WITHIN THE WEEK. That would be about eight weeks early, I realized. I ended up spending about 12 hours in the hospital, but fortunately, everything was OK.

This experience was another lesson on how I process overwhelming situations. I went in by myself at 10am, thinking I was going to leave 45 minutes later and didn't actually call Keith until 2:30pm. Why, you may wonder? I did want to make sure I had accurate information to give him, but even more so: I needed to have time with my own emotions first. I needed to cry and to freak out at God first. You know what happens when you let emotions loose? They eventually pass, and you are left with a clarity and rationality that wouldn't have surfaced if you would have stuffed the emotions deep down inside.

Tears aren't a sign of weakness. They are simply part of the process of accepting your current situation. So, the next time you see someone cry, don't tell them to stop. Just hold them close. Eventually, the tears will turn to laughter again.

****

In the spring of 2019, I was on a skype call with Mama.

Mama: I want to come to the US after the baby is born.

Me: That would be awesome! Should we turn it into a fundraising event for the ministry?

Mama: No, I want to come help you care for the baby.

Me: That's super sweet, but...(trying to approach this without being awkward) I don't think we can afford to bring you over here at this time.

Mama: I don't want you to worry about that. I have plans to raise my own funds, and I will buy my ticket.

Me: Are you sure? You already have so much going on; you don't need this added stress.

Mama: It's what families do for each other. I am very happy to do this!

Me: *speechless*

In late spring, someone stole her phone, and her laptop died. The only way I could contact her was through her son. I messaged him about my hospital stay, and he wrote back in the middle of the night, (his time):

S: "I'm sorry; Mama's sleeping. I'm not able to reach her at this time.

Me: Oh, I knew it was late! I wasn't expecting either of you to respond at this time!

S: Oh, she told me anytime I got news from you about the baby, that

I needed to let her know right away.

Me: *speechless*

We sent her money for a new laptop a little while later, and I asked if she got a new one yet. She didn't respond for a few days and then said, "Sorry for the late response; I was too busy selling melons!" (one of her fundraisers to come see us). I just shook my head, wondering what I had done to deserve her!

****

I know it doesn't always happen, but I wondered whether I would know it if my water broke or if I would miss it somehow. As it turns out, it's not something that you can ignore. My water broke in the early hours of July 23rd, and I have never seen Keith get out of bed so fast when I frantically whispered what was going on.

We had planned for a C-section in the next week or so, because the baby still wasn't measuring average, and the doctor felt the baby could be better cared for outside of the womb at that point. Though we were expecting to meet our baby soon, we were still in shock that the baby wanted to come this early naturally!

****

Did you know the phases of the moon can bring on the labor process? We found that to be absolutely true because a lot of moms delivered early on that day; we were thankful to get a room on the correct floor! And Lucas' physical appearance showed us that we had the wrong due date; the doctor said the way his skin looked is characteristic of 34 weeks, not 36 weeks. It turns out that he was measuring small because his due date should have been around Labor Day, not around August 20th. Thus, Lucas was actually six weeks early.

After a whirlwind C-section experience where the C-section techs had me cracking up with their jokes, I heard Lucas' weak cry and got to see him briefly before they whisked him off to the NICU. I felt bad for Keith; he wasn't sure if he should stay with me or go with Lucas! I sent him off with Lucas because I wanted one of us to be in the loop.

Our little man was 4lbs 4oz and 17 inches long. At one point in his 3-week NICU stay, his weight dropped to 3lb 13oz, and I was terrified to hold him. All of my doubts rose steadily to the surface, especially on the day when a social worker introduced herself to me. I remember looking at her with a "deer in the headlights" look, feeling incredibly vulnerable. She was very kind; she reassured me that there was nothing wrong and that she just wanted to provide me with some resources to help me in my physical uniqueness. I appreciated that; I just wish the hospital had given me a heads-up beforehand.

****

Lucas' NICU stay was a rollercoaster ride, full of so many ups and downs. The doctors and nurses told us to get comfortable with him in the NICU until his due date. I guess that's the default answer to the never-ending question of "When will my baby go home?"

When Lucas was a week old, I posted this on social media:

'I've found it surprisingly easy to speak Scripture over [Lucas]. Verses that have meant a lot to me take on much more meaning when I think of the power they can have over his life.

One of the verses that keeps coming to mind is Zechariah 4:10 - "Do not despise the days of small beginnings." 'Small' is the story of Lucas' life right now. 'Small' is the reason he's in the NICU and won't leave for at least another week or two. "Small/underdeveloped" is the description of several of his systems. Everything is there and functioning; it all just needs TIME to grow and develop.

It's not going to end with "small," but "small" is our reality right now with him. As much as I want to bring him home, I don't want to despise his time in the NICU. I don't want to say that real life begins once he's home. I want to get every little bit of what this experience has to offer. I want to be teachable in this time full of unknowns. After all, if it just takes faith the size of a mustard seed (which is super SMALL) to move mountains, surely I can handle that!'

It's no surprise that "small beginnings" wound its way into the title of this book! The period of "chaos" mentioned in the subtitle started right around the time of Lucas' birth. Small beginnings would absolutely be the theme moving forward.

****

Let me just sing the praises of NICU nurses, but also nurses in general. They have so many hats they need to wear, and they wear the hats with such grace.

I remember one day that the NICU nurses were bustling around, preparing for a baby to be admitted. The baby's umbilical cord came out before the head, which is never a good sign. The mom had to be rushed into surgery, and the nurse had to hop on the gurney with fingers firmly pushing the umbilical cord back into the birth canal. The baby ended up never being admitted to the NICU; he/she was fine! I was in awe of the competence, the speed, and the confidence with which these people accomplished their various tasks.

One silver lining of Lucas' NICU stay was that the nurses could help me find ways to care for Lucas. Remember that I never babysat before this? That also implies that I never changed a diaper before! One nurse in particular had the talent of teaching me while making me laugh at the same time. The nurses helped me brainstorm holding and feeding techniques and just provided overall encouragement that I was going to be a great mom.

The nurses also stepped into the role of nurturing when we couldn't be there. I'd typically go in the morning and stay for about six hours, then come back in the evening after Keith got home from work. The nurses reminded me to get rest at night because once Lucas came home, rest would be trickier to find. I remember there was a day or two when Lucas was the only baby in the NICU. One night, the nurse finished up her tasks and noticed Lucas was wide awake, so she sat and rocked him for a while. That made me breathe a deep sigh of relief. I had to keep telling myself that mom guilt feels true, but it is actually a lie.

It's a lie that if I didn't spend all my time with Lucas in the NICU that I'd be a bad mom. The truth was that I needed to take care of myself, too, so I could be prepared for his homecoming.

It's a lie that Lucas was alone when we were not with him. The truth is that God will never leave him or forsake him and may show up in the form of another person. This is only one reason out of so many that Keith and I need to point Lucas to Jesus continually, because we cannot meet all his needs ourselves.

It's a lie that I'm not going to be a good mom because of my physical limitations. The truth is that God's mercies are new every morning, and He will restore the years the locusts have eaten.

****

I've heard it said that you love your spouse even more deeply after you have kids, and I'd have to say that's very true. Keith stepped up right away in the NICU. He took Lucas' temperature regularly and was not one bit squeamish about changing diapers. He was way more confident about maneuvering Lucas and his wires around than I was. Before we got the hang of helping Lucas drink from a bottle, the nurses were impressed with how Keith fed him. He absolutely was my rock in the first few weeks of Lucas' life.

I am so thankful that Keith and I were married almost three years before we entered parenthood. I believe the foundation that those three years laid is what enabled us to still be a couple today.

NOTES

[1] Magic Eye Inc. 1995. *Magic Eye Gallery.* Andrews McMeel Publishing.

[2] Halverson, Gary . 2001. *Friends.* Television. National Broadcasting Company.

Eight

Love's Painful Price

On Day 20 of Lucas' NICU stay, I found any sense of positivity slipping away. I felt caged and frustrated. He was supposed to come home the day before, but he had another heart rate dip that restarted the clock. He needed to be alarm-free for five days, and the morning of Day 4 quickly turned to Day 0. The good news was that he recovered quickly, so he was improving. And I really didn't want to take home a monitor like some parents have to, so I knew he was where he needed to be.

Still, I found myself thinking about just taking him home. After all, he's my son, isn't he? Can they really stop me? My rational thinking quickly chimed in with a resounding, "Yes, they CAN stop you, and they would!" I didn't want to start motherhood with any kind of police record, so I relented.

I just couldn't shake the restlessness in my spirit. I texted someone that I hit a wall and spent the morning trying to figure out how to scale it. The nurses were doing everything they could, and I was grateful for their efforts. One nurse in particular could make me laugh, and I was thankful she was the one who had to break the news of a longer NICU stay.

Around 1:00, I decided I needed to go run some errands to get my mind off the current situation, so I kissed Lucas and headed out. I came home around 2:00, logged into Facebook, and stepped away for five minutes. I came back to three life-altering messages.

G: MICHELLE, I HAVE BAD NEWS

[Son]: an audio clip

BK, who finally shed some light on the situation: 'It's with great sadness that I inform you [of] the passing of [Mama] today in an accident.

I am so relieved I didn't listen to the audio recording until a year later. All Mama's son said was, "Mom's gone, Michelle. She's dead." I'm sure that's all he could get out. As the only son closest to the accident's location, he had to identify her body. That act alone must sap a person of energy, thoughts, and words.

I remember feeling like I was going to faint. Then I shook my head and said, "This is absurd. This didn't happen," so I forced myself to do some mundane chores. Sending emails would send news of a tragedy packing, right? Washing dishes would wash away waves of grief, wouldn't it? Slowly, the news sank in. I had to wonder if my spirit knew that something wasn't right, and maybe that's why I felt off all day.

****

My Mennonite background ingrained in me the duty that I had to the world. In my church growing up, this was jokingly referred to as 'the Mennonite verse: "...make it your ambition to lead a quiet life: You should mind your own business and work with your hands" from 1 Thessalonians 4:11. In other words, I am supposed to show up to the world, do my work, and shut up. When Mama came into my life, though, she turned that philosophy all on its head.

She told me from Day 1 that I had a story that needed to be shared. I had conquered so much in my life that would give so many people hope. I didn't have to be obnoxious about it, but I could hold my head up high and proclaim with confidence what God had done in my life. She was my loudest cheerleader, and now she was just...gone? It couldn't be true.

For the next hour or so, I couldn't talk. I could not speak the words out loud that Mama was dead. Instead, I texted the words, and each text was met with disbelief, shock, and some minor denial: "Are you sure?" While I understood the denial, because I had just experienced it myself, a rage rose in me. "Do you think I'd share something like this without being sure?!"

In Season 4 of *The Chosen*, there is a death of someone very close to one of the disciples[1]. Watching these episodes five years after Mama's death, I had some visceral reactions. The disciple couldn't stop pacing in one scene, and I couldn't stop pacing when I heard that Mama was gone. It's as though my body knew it had to do something, so my mind wouldn't explode in grief. A few episodes later, Lazarus was raised from the dead, and this disciple threw all his fury at Jesus. At the end of his tirade, Jesus said something gently to him, and the disciple yelped and threw himself down as though that was the only sound and action he had left in him. Jesus didn't reprimand him or shame the disciple for his outburst, but when Love Himself meets raw and searing grief, it brings the grieving person to a primitive state. When Mama died, I wanted to run and hide from God. I didn't want all that He was offering me because He could have stopped all this...and He didn't. But deep down, I knew that all I could do was yelp and fall at His feet because where else could I go?

✳✳✳✳✳✳✳✳✳✳

Lucas was released from the NICU a few days after Mama died, and for once, I saw some silver lining. If Lucas had been released before the accident, I would have had no time to myself to grieve. At least I had 48 hours or so to process without being the primary caregiver for him. The night before he was released, Keith and I had to go into the NICU for some instruction since he needed a vitamin supplement and some other special care. I hadn't shared anything about

Mama's passing with the NICU staff, so I was desperately trying to hold in tears while taking in important information. I'm pretty sure that translated into yelping and falling at Jesus' feet in the spiritual realm.

Also knowing that Mama would never be able to visit and help care for Lucas like she was planning was a realization that was equal parts searing pain and dull numbness. I didn't even get the chance to take one dang picture of the two of them. I felt all of the things and none of the things, and I didn't know which extreme was worse. Eventually, I imagined her saying to me in her blunt, English-as-her-third-language way, "It's OK if you miss me, but if your grief keeps you from caring for Lucas, I will beat you!" She never minced words, and that thought actually made me laugh. I went back to that encouragement a lot in the first few months. I knew she would want me to forge a way forward and to cling to Jesus with everything I had in me.

****

Before my world came crashing down, I was proud of how my body was championing motherhood. While my mind was flooded with doubts and anxieties, my body was stepping up to the challenge of providing for Lucas. I had nurses tell me some full-term mothers weren't producing as much milk as I was. They even started sending milk home to freeze, so it wouldn't go bad. Yes! Finally, something that came easily for me in this new journey!

I didn't notice it at first, but about a week after Mama's death, it became apparent that my milk supply was tanking. I stopped pumping completely about three weeks later and switched to formula. At first, I berated my body. Everything else was letting me down; why aren't you supporting me?! Then I felt the Holy Spirit gently remind me, "Your mind, spirit, and body are all connected. You need to let each part of you grieve the way it needs to." I let out a deep sigh and wondered if it was my body thanking me for compassion. I heard somewhere that grief is love with no place to go. Grief is the painful side of love; it's the price we need to pay for the privilege of loving another person.

****

Grief changes people and may lead them to actions they wouldn't normally consider. It is customary in this country that the dead are buried where they were born; however, the staff at the ministry wondered if they could bury her on ministry property. It seemed only fitting. Mama was one of the few followers of Jesus in her family, and seeing as the ministry had a focus on Jesus, her family wasn't enthusiastic. As a group from the ministry approached her family to have a discussion, they were met by actual flying stones. The family forbade the staff from attending the funeral and any other customary gathering.

There were some questionable decisions made in Mama's immediate family as well, and I say none of this in judgment. Mama was a true matriarch and kept so many areas of life afloat for her family. Her absence left a gaping vacuum with her family grasping at anything to fill it. Interestingly enough, she had been preparing for a successor to her ministry all this time because she knew this ministry had to continue without her. She had named a family member as successor.

Not long before the accident, this family member had finished school with a degree that prepared him for this leadership role, and though he was professionally qualified, he wasn't ready personally. Who could blame him? He also didn't have as much experience working with Westerners as Mama, and several individuals on the US board seemed to take note of that.

****

Let's pause and go back a few years. In the spring of 2017, Mama officially asked if I would form a 501(c)3 non-profit organization to provide funding for the ministry. I dragged my feet for so long because I didn't know the first thing about starting an organization, and the thought of paperwork and legal fees seemed daunting and overwhelming. Eventually, I warmed up to the idea, and the process ended up being easier than I originally thought.

I had to choose a board of directors, and as obvious as it sounds, you only know the people you know. As I considered the roles of the board and the people in my life, I slowly wrote down names. When it came to one member, I felt the Holy Spirit say, "You know the two of you are going to have a lot of differences, right?" I said, "Well, that helps groups grow, and we're adults, so we can handle it."

That was the most naive thought I could have ever had.

****

Remember back in chapter 4 when I said some Americans promised to send money to Mama but then never did? She and I had a lot of talks about Western missionary influence. Her son also worked at the hospital, and he and an American had the same role, yet the American got paid THREE. TIMES. what her son did. She asked me why that was. I did know the reason the hospital would give - higher costs of living in the US, even though the American was living in this particular country - but I didn't have the heart to tell her, so I just said I didn't know.

After my time in the Land of Transformation in 2014, I was introduced to *Missions Dilemma*[2], a series of messages hosted by Steve Saint, son of Nate Saint, whose father was one of the missionaries killed in the *End of the Spear*[3] story. The purpose of these messages is for Westerners to hear from the people they typically go to serve - Africans, Asians, Indians, etc. How are the Westerners doing in their service? What could they improve on? It was such an eye-opener and so sobering.

Steve talks about the purpose of missions:

- **to know** the message
- **to go** to people

- **to show** the people the message and the significance it can have in their lives
- **to blow** away and let the local people take it from there

I can think of at least one titan agency in the Western missionary world that could use this lesson. Sure, the people on the ground may move on, but more people take their place. In addition, the agency itself seems to have its tentacles pretty firmly embedded in the way they feel the Church should behave around the world. Buuuut, I digress. The crucial point in the series is that Westerners are harming a lot more than they are healing around the world. Westerners must learn that intention doesn't always equal impact. People might have the purest of intentions, but if they sit and listen to the people they go to serve, they may learn their impact was unhelpful at best, and harmful at worst.

The main thing Mama and I talked about from *Mission Dilemma* is that no matter where Westerners go in the world, they come in power, simply because they are Westerners. That is all the more reason for Westerners to humble themselves, sit at the locals' feet, and be eager to learn from them, rather than the other way around. Locals tend to be quiet when Westerners are in the room, so Westerners should learn to be the first to listen and the last to speak up, so locals can have confidence in their own experience and wisdom.

****

Let's head back to 2019. Mama and I were looking at the "know, go, show, blow" concept, and we were in agreement that the US organization eventually had to "blow away" - we had to work ourselves out of a job, in a sense. Mama was extremely proactive in trying to come up with ways for the ministry to be self-sufficient, and she was highly successful. For example, the ministry was growing a lot of its own food.

Mama had told me there is a tendency for Western missionaries to help people in her country start up an organization and then slowly creep in to the point where they take it over. What she said next gave me chills: "I appreciate that you all want to help, but if there is ever any sense that the ministry may be taken from me, I will cut off all ties." That definitely put the fear of God in me to know that she wasn't joking.

I wasn't worried about myself and several other board members. The majority of us were in agreement that Mama ran the show, and we took orders from her. However, even before Mama's accident, I was wrestling with the actions of the other board members. I was worried they might want the American side to play a bigger part in the ministry than necessary. My only regret in this whole fiasco is that I never called a meeting with the whole group + Mama to discuss the drama. I used Mama as a crutch because whatever she said, they listened to. They never listened to me, even when Mama reminded them of my place. After the accident, they had even less reason to listen to me.

A week before the accident, I had my last phone call with Mama. I was frustrated and tired of not being treated as I felt I deserved in my position as President. Don't get me wrong; I didn't want to lord my position over anyone, but I was the person on the board with the longest relationship to the ministry, and I felt that should mean something. She sympathized with me; it turns out that she was being undermined in her role in her part of the world, even though this was her vision in the first place. I really wondered if I should step down. I vividly remember what she said to me, because I clung to it fiercely for several months: "I can't force you to stay on the board, but I feel that if you were to step down, God would have told me who was to take your place. I haven't heard anything from Him."

****

After the period of intense grief subsided, I tried hard to get back into my role as President. I even called in a mediator to help me have a discussion with one board member. The meeting seemed successful at first, but within a few weeks, it seemed that the familiar pattern of feeling undermined and overlooked resumed.

I noticed that this drama was placing unnecessary stress on my home life. I was lashing out at Keith who did nothing to deserve it. I was impatient with Lucas, who was just starting in life. I had to do some soul-searching to find out where my true priorities were. Something had to change.

In the end, I stepped down from my role as president and from the board entirely in January 2020. On one hand, I felt immense grief. On the other hand, I felt incredible relief. I felt like I let Mama down, yet I felt that I was doing my part to keep my family whole and healthy.

Through all of this, I have felt Jesus speaking to me: "You have no idea of the depth of the promise that the last will be first. I see all of this more clearly than you do. I feel the sadness more deeply than you do. I love the staff and kids at the ministry more completely than you ever could. I've got this."

As I mentioned in Chapter 1, I'm learning how to lay down discomfort that isn't mine. Apparently this lesson applies in this situation, as well. I need to pass on my discomfort to Jesus, because He is big enough to carry it and wise enough to be able to do something about it.

NOTES

[1] Jenkins, Dallas. 2024. *The Chosen.* Television. 5&2 Studios.

[2] "Missions Dilemma - ITEC | Develop | Train | Equip." 2025. Itecusa.org. 2025. https://itecusa.org/missions-dilemma.

[3] Saint, Steve. 2005. *End of the Spear : A True Story.* Carol Stream, Ill.: Tyndale House Publishers.

Nine

Parenting, Pandemics, and Politics

I wish I had had a few weeks of normal parenting under my belt before grief hit. I wish the first 3 weeks of Lucas' life had been at home rather than in the NICU. I wish I had some semblance of routine in place before my life turned itself upside down.

I already felt less than adequate as a mom before grief intruded. And when grief barged in, I was even more bewildered about everything. I remember clearly the night before Lucas was discharged. As I received the discharge instructions, I felt like crumbling to the floor in tears rather than taking care of my son because collapsing in tears just seemed so much easier.

I have struggled with confidence for as long as I can remember, and Lucas' first year of life didn't help my confidence level. Let me be clear, though. The problem with my confidence was NOT about Lucas. He didn't ask to be conceived. He didn't ask to be brought into a world where friends die in accidents or from shingles that attack your organs rather than manifest as a rash, as it does in many cases. Oh yeah, I forgot to mention that five weeks after Mama was killed, another dear friend died. I was truly floundering that first year.

In Lucas' first year of life, he was a baby doing his baby stuff, and he was a cute one whom I loved dearly! It was and still is my goal with the help of Jesus to always speak life to Lucas and about Lucas. I want to be clear that he was never the issue. Also, a full circle moment happened when he was a baby. Remember the little girl from Chapter 7 who ran away from my class? Soon after Lucas was born, she messaged me for my address; she had made a blanket for Lucas! He still sleeps with it five years later. That encounter brought a sweet smile to my spirit.

Back to the topic at hand - the issue was and always has been about me. Years of shame, comparison, and not feeling comfortable in my own skin hadn't gone away, and I experienced these same feelings again when I parented Lucas. It felt like a vicious cycle.

In early 2020, I was re-reading *1000 Gifts*.[1] In the first chapter, Ann Voskamp talks about how the Israelites ate something that was literally translated to "What is it?" They had to "eat the mystery." While I didn't need to eat anything weird, I got the impression this was God's invitation to me to live the mystery. To trust that the mystery of parenting is a good one to be solved a day at a time. To believe that Lucas really was created for me and that all he needs is for me to show up. To walk in faith that God, the Ultimate Parent, will always parent me and show me the way.

****

A month or so after Mama died, we sang a song at church with a line about fear and depression needing to bow to Jesus. I wholeheartedly agreed with that sentiment, but in that moment, I felt unsettled by the message it sent.

I felt unsettled because fear and depression are seen as negative things, and yet...I was grieving. To an extent, fear and depression go along with grief. These feelings are part of the process. So, is grief wrong, too, if those other emotions are? Of course not! I don't think the song is implying that either. My question was, what if God was working through the fear and depression to bring about His purposes? And if that was the case, should I want them to go away right away?

I remember reading in Jeremiah where the captives were told to bloom where they were planted - to get jobs, get married and have kids. In captivity?! In the book *Hinds Feet on High Places*[2], Much Afraid is given the companions of Sorrow and Suffering to help her complete her journey. She hated these companions at first, but at the end of her journey, she actually grew to have a deep appreciation for them.

Losing someone dear to you is like the amputation of a limb. You can't recover or get over it. You can only adapt. I saw how God had been helping me adapt in ways only possible through Him.

I still ached, though. I felt phantom pain with this amputation. The loss of friends wasn't a season that would pass. This was life. Daily, I needed to wrap my mind around the fact that I would never talk to my two dear friends in this life again. While this loss wasn't a season, I had to grieve that my friendships **were** a season. A season that ended way too abruptly, way too soon. TobyMac said it so well:

Some things are only for a season
and just the thought of letting go
...[brings] you to your knees.
(See the Light)[3]

As much as I wanted this ache to go away from the perspective of being on my knees, I felt the pull to bloom where I was planted. Not to let fear and depression overwhelm me but to use them to pull me closer to the Ultimate Comforter. Not to wish the pain away, but to hang on to the Ultimate Healer.

****

Where was I planted in those early months of Lucas' life? I was plopped into the Wild West of one-handed parenting. When I was pregnant, I worked with an occupational therapist who assured me I would do well. I just needed to take it slowly and befriend progress that came at the speed of turtle. I was so thankful that she was willing to work with me after Lucas arrived; she even came to our house! Her insights were invaluable, and she reassured me again that I would do well. Her main advice to me was, "Plan all the steps before starting anything!"

That strategy - while effective - often left me overwhelmed, and I didn't go many places alone with Lucas as a result. Keith was the main caretaker out in public, but even then, I could see my influence on Lucas' life. After church one day, I went off to talk to someone while Keith held Lucas. When I came back, he said, "Lucas was getting antsy, and when he saw you coming back, he calmed down right away." I guess what I said in Chapter 7 does ring true - when the littles feel safe and secure with someone, not much else matters. Somehow, even in the messiness of grief, Lucas still saw me as a safe haven.

I remember the day I was determined to take him for a walk by myself. It was 70 degrees in March; we had to get out! The preparation was stressful, but my friend "Progress via Patience" urged me forward. I was adamant about giving Lucas the childhood he deserved, and the walk was successful!

****

When I said "March" in the last section, I was referring to March of 2020. Around the time of the successful walk, I was finally starting to breathe a little deeper, a little easier. I remember on our last day of church before everything closed down due to COVID, that Lucas was surrounded by little kids, and they were all making him belly laugh. I thought, "Maybe we can start moving forward." In grief, you don't move on from something; you move forward with the loss and do your best to make the loss impact your life for the better.

One direction we faced was another journey for Lucas; he was born with a condition that, while not life-threatening, did involve surgery as a solution. His first surgery was scheduled for March 19th, 2020. I remember asking the surgeon at the pre-op appointment in

February how often surgeries get canceled. She said, "Oh, it would have to be something pretty major for me to cancel a surgery."

Well, those were famous last words! In the days leading up to March 19th, I began to wonder if we would have to cancel the surgery because of this Coronavirus thing. Sure enough, the surgeon called me herself on Monday, March 16th. We weren't sure when the surgery would be rescheduled, and it hit me hard when I heard her say, "Let's face it. I'm going to get the virus at some point, and I would hate for him not to be able to come in for his follow-up appointments." She resigned herself to the fact that she would get sick, yet she still showed up to work every day.

I wanted to cry as I hung up the phone. Not because his surgery was canceled. No - that actually showed God at work. Originally, the surgery was supposed to be in the first week of March. What would it be like to be in the middle of the recovery process and not be able to see the surgeon for follow-up? BAD. Again, I was in awe of how God works.

I wanted to cry because I do not know how medical professionals do it. I do not know how they show up every day, potentially staring death in the face on any normal day and even more magnified in 2020. I don't know how they remain calm and confident in their abilities, even when they don't know exactly what is going on. Medical professionals are rockstars, plain and simple.

****

Emotions ran high for all of us in those early days of the pandemic. I mentioned in Chapter 7 that Keith and I planned on deviating from the traditional parenting methods our Christian circles tend to endorse. One of those deviations was that we were not going to discipline Lucas for having meltdowns.

Society embraces us when we express "positive" emotions like happiness but frowns when we express "negative" emotions like sadness or anger. The thing is, no emotion is bad. Emotions are there to tell us when things are going right or wrong and what we can do about it. The key is to learn appropriate ways to express them.

Don't get me wrong; our plan is never to give in to tantrums, but there is a difference between tantrums and meltdowns. Tantrums end as soon as the child gets the desired object. Meltdowns are all about overstimulation, and once kids start screaming and crying, they literally cannot stop until the internal storm passes. When Lucas has big emotions, he's learning how to deal with them, and that doesn't come naturally. As parents, Keith and I attempt to bring our calm into his chaos, and our energy into his exhaustion. Studies show that when children are allowed to express their emotions in a safe environment, they can move on from the intensity much more easily.

****

I said all that to say, the same goes for adults, too. No emotion is off-limits, but we need a safe place where we can unload. If I keep pushing my emotions to the side, they're going to keep popping up until they're dealt with properly.

It was at this point in late March of 2020 that I allowed myself to reflect on what I had dealt with over the last eight months.

-I was a NICU mama for three weeks.

-Pretty much right after Lucas was in the NICU, I lost two dear friends in five weeks to freak accidents and illnesses.

-We had multiple appointments to try to figure Lucas out, which all amounted to nothing, and he was OK other than the necessary surgeries.

-We finally got a surgery date scheduled.

-A freaking VIRUS came to the US and turned everyone's plans upside down, including the surgery.

I was able to find things to be thankful for in everything that I mentioned above, but my soul was still so exhausted. I felt God telling me, "The grace you want to extend to Lucas to let him feel his emotions through - you need to extend that same grace to yourself, too."

Giving thanks in hard times is so important. It keeps your perspective in a good place. But if you don't give your pain the attention it deserves, it's like bandaging a wound continuously so that it doesn't get the air it needs to heal.

Eventually, I admitted that I was depressed. I was very careful how I scheduled things, so I wouldn't overdo it. I found it interesting that everyone else felt forced to quarantine when I'd been doing so for the last eight months. In an interview,[4] Jim Carrey said that when you are depressed, you need "deep rest."

I realized that I needed to do a better job of feeling my pain. I needed to do a better job of letting my emotions move freely through me, so I could be healed a little bit deeper. This didn't give me the excuse to treat people rudely and lash out. But this admission of depression did give me permission to find a safe place to let loose.

I think all along I'd been worried that if I let loose, I wouldn't be able to stop. I wouldn't be able to go about my daily routine. The more I thought about it though, the more I compared myself to a child who is just EXHAUSTED. If I let all my tears and rage out, maybe then I'd "fall asleep." Maybe I would actually be able to feel grateful instead of just going through the motions. Maybe "feeling deeply" was the key to finding my "deep rest."

I chose not to go on meds, though I am NOT against meds in any way. I just figured the majority of my depression came from the list of events I posted above, not from any serious chemical imbalance.

Once I was able to be honest with myself about my emotional state of being, my spirit felt a bit lighter. I realized the lightness I felt wasn't insignificant, given that we were in the midst of a global pandemic.

****

A friend of mine said that when we were still just hearing about this mysterious virus, she wondered if this was going to turn into a reckoning for the global Church. Would we face our messiness and come together in humility to repair and restore damage done in years past - maybe even centuries past? Or were we just going to dig our heels in and claim our "rights" and our "rightness" in everything?

I read something on social media one day that said, "If you aren't freaked out by this [COVID] situation, you're not a real person." I'm sure it was meant as a joke, but it got me thinking, nonetheless.

For me personally, quarantine was a blessing in disguise. Because I already worked online, our school continued on without a hitch. Keith had to take two months off, and unemployment checks started coming in right away. Nothing really changed for us. After experiencing those insane last eight months, quarantine was a time to intentionally gather my thoughts, take time for myself to breathe, and feel absolutely no pressure to perform. Those months in quarantine were so instrumental in helping me start to come out of "The Valley of the Shadow of Death," and I was so thankful to see little shoots of life start growing in my heart again.

We were, however, prepared in that we lead a simple life and live below our means. We aren't the kind of people to buy the first things that catch our eye because we "need" them. We weren't disappointed when salons, movie theaters, etc. were closed. The lifestyle we lead was not affected by this situation.

I wore a mask. Not all the time, but if I went somewhere where it was required, I didn't complain; I simply wore one. I saw it as a sign of respect, even though people may have lumped me into the "sheeple" category. I think people coined the "sheeple" label because they wanted to describe those people as being fearful and unable to think for themselves. On the contrary, I felt like I was honoring God and others by wearing a mask and social distancing.

Of course, there were some fears among mask wearers: fear for their health and safety as well as that of those they love, fear for how school was going to look for their kids and whether they would have a good educational experience under these circumstances, fear for their financial status, as well.

I wonder if there was fear in the other camp, too. The camp of conspiracy theories and shouts for freedom. The camp where loving your neighbors - the "sheeple" - looked like laughing at them. I've heard it said that anger is fear's bodyguard. Was there anything under this anger? Did these fears look like this: "My lifestyle is being challenged, and I don't know how to handle it?" "I have to work from home now, and I don't know what to do with my kids." "I don't have money for the fun things I used to."?

Fear makes you vulnerable. Anger gives you energy and something to cling to. I wish we had all been able to set aside our surface emotions about this virus and come together in honesty, talking about how we really felt, and like my friend said, "Begin to repair and restore damages done."

****

The spring of 2020 continued. Lucas' first surgery date was rescheduled for early June, so we were anxiously anticipating everything about it. He was growing and developing well, albeit at his own pace. Because he had been in the NICU, the hospital automatically put us in touch with Early Intervention. An interventionist had come to our house when Lucas was two months old, and since he was on target developmentally, they marked us down to receive checklists every two months to make sure his development stayed on track.

In May 2020, the familiar fears returned. Lucas was ten months old and wasn't crawling yet; he barely tolerated being on his tummy and couldn't go from lying to sitting yet. Was I doing enough in motherhood? Lucas and I didn't go to a lot of places just the two of us; as I mentioned before, that was the case even before the pandemic. Our driveway was a million miles away from our house, and schlepping him in his car seat the whole way to the car was not an activity

I enjoyed. As a result, we spent a lot of time at home, and as I saw more and more people shake off quarantine doldrums and resume their lives, I wondered why I didn't feel rested enough to join them. Why did the fears have to come back?

"At home" didn't even mean the whole house; we were specifically in our living room downstairs because I couldn't climb stairs with Lucas. I found I was constantly asking myself if he was missing out on stuff because of me. Was he losing out on learning opportunities because of me? What were infants supposed to be learning, anyway? I didn't want to be the mom who says to his kindergarten teacher, "How will you be preparing my son for Harvard?" I mean, come on. Those parents frustrate me to no end. I wanted to find a good place between enrichment from adults and discovery on his own.

All that speculation aside, I tried to focus on what was in front of me. It's easier now in hindsight! In the span of a month, he went from being placed in a lying or sitting position to initiating those positions himself, as well as crawling! All of this happened as he was recovering from surgery, by the way. I saw a little boy who was very inquisitive. When he got his hands on a new object, meant for him or not, he didn't just shove it into his mouth right away anymore. He would turn it over, pass it from hand to hand, squeeze it, pull at it, and examine it ever so intently. I saw a little boy who loved being social, making faces at us, squealing at us, and delighting in peekaboo.

One face that Lucas and I made to each other specifically was a snooty face with lips puckered up. After Keith and Lucas returned from the hospital after his first surgery, I anxiously looked in the car seat, wondering how my baby was dealing with this strange experience. As soon as Lucas saw me, he made a snooty face, and I knew we were going to be OK. His next surgery was scheduled for early December.

****

COVID eventually caught us in October 2020. I was exhausted and experienced chest tightness, and Keith lost his sense of taste and smell, but otherwise, we were OK. I remember lying on the floor one day; I'm pretty sure I fell asleep for a few minutes. I woke up to silence, and everyone with toddlers knows that silence is never a good sign. Right away, I noticed the baby gate was open at the steps, and sure enough, Lucas was chilling at the top of the steps, looking quite proud of himself! I wasn't sure how I was going to get him down, but he willingly plopped onto my lap, and we scooted downstairs that way.

We didn't bother getting Lucas tested for COVID because we just figured he got it from us. Keith noticed he had a slight fever one night, but otherwise, Lucas didn't seem bothered by anything. Looking back, it would have been super helpful if we had gotten him tested, but as I said in a previous chapter, we can only make decisions with the information we have right in front of us.

****

A few days before his surgery, Lucas tested positive for COVID at the mandatory hospital check. It was at least five weeks after Keith and I tested positive, and we learned - at that point, at least - a person could still test positive for up to twelve weeks.

I wasn't angry at the hospital. This hospital is a leading hospital in many areas, so if the staff went down, lots of lives would be affected. I did feel something snap in me, though. I realized that if someone comes to me professing faith over fear, throwing caution to the wind, "you only live once," I don't feel safe with that person. Throughout the last few months of 2020, I unfriended people on social media for whom I had previously had the utmost respect. People who taught me a lot about the Holy Spirit and walking in the gifts of the Spirit. But the tone of their posts in 2020 just repulsed me. I realized that I don't care how much a person walks in power or confidence in all that God can do in their life. If their walk is not clothed in love and humility, considering other people better than themselves, I don't have time for them anymore.

I couldn't believe the following stories I heard throughout 2020:

Someone wears a mask to a church service. Another church member calls them names with a rude hand gesture.

Someone invites a friend to her house. The friend says she will wear a mask. The host tells the friend not to bother coming.

A friend's loved one dies of COVID. A family member says it was "just their time to go" and refused to wear a mask at the funeral, ignoring the request of both the church as well as the deceased's spouse.

All of those stories were unrelated to me, but they still left me reeling. The story that actually happened to me is the root of why I don't see certain family members regularly anymore. To me, this event really "takes the cake" for the depths of absurdity to which members of the global Church have lowered themselves.

There was a significant family event that took place in the spring of 2020, and after many hard discussions, Keith and I agreed not to attend the event. We were in a global pandemic, after all, and we also didn't want Lucas' first surgery to be rescheduled again. Some members of the family were very understanding. Other family members didn't understand, and rather than communicating their frustrations with us, they chose to go the route of a faith-based family counseling session in June, a few months after the event took place.

It began with someone accusing me of being the reason for my little family's absence at the event.

"Thanks for throwing me under the bus from the very start," I shot back. (I admit, I didn't help the situation by choosing the tone I did in reply.)

"I didn't throw you under the bus!" he barked.

Thankfully, other family members and the counselor stood up for me and agreed that the accusation was out of line. The session went downhill from there. The counselor, a mild-mannered, soft-spoken person, truly did his best to try to untangle the mess that was in front of him. Honestly, though, the members in the group should have gone to counseling years ago for other matters; this event was only the tip of the iceberg. It was clear there wasn't much the counselor could do, though he tried, and I appreciated it. Certain members stood up for me at other points in the session, and that helped alleviate some of my stress.

The fact was crystal-clear to me, though, that those who scheduled the session had a goal in mind - to get the counselor to see the "right" side of the issue and to have the counselor make everyone else see it, too. That's not the point of counseling, though. The point of counseling is to come to the conclusion that it's impossible to change another person. We can only change ourselves. Thankfully, the counselor saw through that goal and did his best to give everyone a voice in the session.

I left that counseling session and all of 2020 with the thought ringing in my ear, "How in the name of all things holy did we as a society and as a global Church get to where we are now?!"

****

I speak monthly with a friend from Germany, and in 2020, she shared that she was reading books about American presidents and learning many fascinating facts along the way. That piqued my interest. Since Lucas was born, I have read more than I ever have in my life because I've just been so hungry for stimulating thoughts and discussions, and books seemed the easiest solution.

Pondering this question with curiosity, "How did we get to where we are now?" I began my own history journey. At the time of this writing, my friend jokes that I beat her at her own game - I'm further along than she is. I started with George Washington and am currently reading about World War II. I never expected the journey would be this much fun and that the author of Ecclesiastes was so right - There is nothing new under the sun!

****

There are a lot of believers in Jesus who cry out with every "new" historic development that it's the end of the world. They say that the world keeps getting worse, and it's only a matter of time until Jesus comes back. I really wish people would go on a similar history journey as the one I am going on because they would see the following:

-Back in John Adams' day (our second president), people beat each other with canes in the Senate. Doesn't that sound like our current Congress situation, where division gets more public feedback than unity?

-Back in John Adams' day, there were competing newspapers that called the others demeaning names and said the others essentially produced fake news. This is absolutely our current situation!

-Our fourth president James Madison, known as the Father of the Constitution, found loopholes in his own document when the document went against his wishes! There are multiple current debates about what relevance the Constitution has in the US.

There is nothing new under the sun.

****

Here's where I want to camp out: James Monroe, our fifth president, came up with this document called the Monroe Doctrine. It essentially warned Europe not to continue with colonization in the Western hemisphere, and at first glance, that sounds amazing. Colonization has left a bad taste in many mouths, so we should absolutely put a stop to it. However, what the doctrine implied was that the US could do whatever it wanted in the Western Hemisphere, which included expansion of its own.

One could argue, "Well, the US hasn't expanded beyond the fifty states, so is that doctrine really a big deal?" I will counter argue that YES, it is a big deal! It's a big deal because the expansion to include all fifty states caused a lot of upheaval and death. The impact of this doctrine is also a big deal because it has allowed hubris to seep into our way of thinking. Remember that word from Chapter 2? The "dangerous overconfidence" that we have about our worldview? I think the danger lies in the fact that we often don't realize how confident we are and where our confidence lies regarding our impact on the rest of the world. This hubris has led to:

-the creation of boarding schools for Native American children, where the goal was to "kill the Indian to save the man," a quote by Richard Pratt, a founder of at least one of these schools. Children in these schools were forced to drop their home culture and religion and adopt the customs and religion of the white man. Some of those schools only closed as late as the 1970s.[5]

-creative methods to keep black people inferior to white people: Did you know cities and suburbs were designed like they are on purpose? The actual goal was to keep black people and white people apart from each other. In the 1920s, there was a wealthy suburban area for black people in Tulsa, OK, and white supremacists went on a 2-day killing spree to decimate that reality.[6] A current-day horror is that there is a prison in Louisiana that has mostly black inmates, and the inmates are forced to pick cotton.[7]

And finally:

-Christian Nationalism: This is the belief that the US government needs to be Christian, and everyone in the country needs to follow a Christian way of life, whether or not they profess Christianity as a personal faith. Christian Nationalism is the most insidious way that the US is flexing its "dangerously overconfident" muscles. It is the foundation of this nationwide hubris.

I'm baffled because if we want to follow Jesus, we need to understand that He never came to overthrow Rome. He came to serve, to heal, and to love. In some places in the Gospels, it was tough love, for sure, but it was never His aim to force people to do something they didn't want to do. Jesus knew there were consequences to people's actions, but in His decision not to coerce people one way or another, He demonstrated that for pure love to exist, there must be free will. Jesus' harshest words were for people in the religious system of the day, not the "sinners." He drove people out of the temple because they had a different vision than He did. I think, instead of following the Jesus of the Gospels, the adherents of Christian Nationalism worship the Jesus who is to come, who will make everything right in an instant. They fail to realize, though, that it is Jesus who will make everything right; it's not His followers' task to undertake, especially not in His name.

In different places in the Old Testament, it says, "[So and so] was a good king, but he did not remove the high places." While reading this, it's easy to get impatient and say, "Just remove them already. The distinction of 'high place' makes it seem pretty obvious what it is!" I began to get the impression, though, that "high places" are customs or traditions that are so ingrained in our culture that we don't realize they are an issue. Does Christian Nationalism fall under this umbrella? Absolutely.

****

I had to metaphorically pick myself up off the floor after I had that realization. The reason that a lot of Americans don't want to read up on history is that they are afraid the version they will read will contradict the version they learned in school. News flash - it will contradict that version! The version we tend to learn in school is one where the US is painted as either the victor or the victim, never the villain. The "dangerous confidence" that Christian Nationalism gives people allows for that view of history to take place. It allows people to make god into a scapegoat and to say, "Oh, god hates this, so we need to hate this, too and act accordingly." And then to add insult to injury, we say, "But of course we still love the sinner."

I used lowercase 'g' on purpose in the previous paragraph, because the true God will never accept being a scapegoat, so we can arm ourselves with the excuse to hurt people, physically, emotionally, or otherwise. The true God is always and will always be about love, healing, restoration, and wholeness. William Paul Young, author of *The Shack,* encourages us to look at God as a doctor who has the goal to heal patients rather than as a judge who has the goal to condemn criminals[8].

****

Perspective truly makes all of the difference. If we ultimately believe that the sin in our lives is a wound that needs to be healed rather than a crime that needs to be punished, doesn't that help us look at ourselves and the world with more compassion? We would never punish people because they are sick! I've heard, though, that when you worship power (as in the case of Christian Nationalism), concepts like "compassion", "mercy", and "kindness" seem weak.

But they are not weak! Jesus elevating women to meet their potential was not weak! Jesus gathering the children to Himself was not weak! Jesus' declaration to the man on the cross that he would be with Jesus in Paradise was not weak!

It's Christian Nationalism that is weak. The goal of this "movement" is to see every problem as a nail, so they can use god as the hammer. Where is the strength in beating someone down? Where is the strength in pointing fingers at people who are highly aware they are different? Where is the strength in minimizing one's own sin, presumably to "gain heavenly capital" by pointing out someone else's sin? Where is the strength in pointing out the speck in someone else's eye when one's own eyes are oozing with hubris?

At the time of this writing, Lucas is five, and I don't want him to come to Jesus for fire insurance like I did. I don't want him to wonder after every lapse of reason, every poor decision, if God's at the end of His patience with him. In a callback to Chapter 2, I want Lucas to do things out of his LOVE for Jesus, not out of fear of the consequence. It is, after all, God's kindness that leads us to repentance (Romans 2:4).

Let me be clear. If someone aligns with Christian Nationalism, Jesus can be present in this person. I'm not here to say who's in and who's out, as that isn't our job. I do, however, believe that Jesus is not present in the Christian Nationalism movement overall.

****

What's the antidote to hubris, then? How can we rid ourselves of this "high place?"

We can start right with the pronunciation of the word *hubris*! I had seen it before I had heard it, so I imagined it would be pronounced like *debris*, but it's not! The -s is pronounced! I didn't get embarrassed that I didn't know how to pronounce the word; I just chalked it up to "You learn something new every day."

The opposite of *hubris* is *humility*. I like Rick Warren's definition of *humility*: "It's not thinking less of ourselves, it's thinking of ourselves less."[9] It's realizing what I learned in college: "The more I know, the more I realize I don't know." It's embracing the mystery that I mentioned earlier in the chapter, that we're never going to know everything about God in this life and that we have no idea what will happen in the next. Sure, we have several stories of people who have experienced Heaven and have come back to life, but that was only a snapshot. We have zero idea of what all of eternity looks like. Rather than scaring us and having us make up stories so it all makes sense, it should make us curious.

The opposite of *hubris* is found in Philippians 2:3-8. These verses talk about laying aside our own agenda and putting others before ourselves. I can't recall hearing this passage being preached during the pandemic, and I have my opinions as to whether it was coincidental or not! Interestingly enough, verses 8-11 of that chapter talk about what Jesus went through, and only then was He brought to the highest place and given the Name above all names. If we're not careful, we can gloss over the messiness of this life and focus solely on the ease of the next.

Essentially, I believe that the opposite of *hubris* is focusing on the present and going through life with the "I Am," who is eager to heal yesterday's hurt, to reveal the mystery of each moment, and to demonstrate delight in the messiness of the everyday and the mundane. It's as simple as that, but it's the opposite of easy.

NOTES

[1] Voskamp, Ann. 2010. *One Thousand Gifts : A Dare to Live Fully Right Where You Are.* Nashville, Tn: W Publishing Group, An Imprint Of Thomas Nelson.

[2] Hurnard, Hannah. 1993. *Hinds' Feet on High Places.* Destiny Image Pub.

[3] TobyMac. 2018. *See the Light.* Album. Forefront.

[4] "Jim Carrey on Depression: 'Your Body Needs Deep Rest.'" n.d. Www.youtube.com. Accessed April 2, 2025. https://www.youtube.com/shorts/lMQJ2bHeP4c.

[5] McMahon, Sharon. "Taken: Native Boarding Schools in America" – A Series. *Here's Where it Gets Interesting.'* June, 2023. Podcast.

[6] "1921 Tulsa Race Massacre - Tulsa Historical Society & Museum." 2018. Www.tulsahistory.org. November 1, 2018. https://tulsahistory.org/exhibit/1921-tulsa-race-massacre/.

[7] "Louisiana Prisoners Demand an End to 'Modern-Day Slavery.'" n.d. The Appeal. https://theappeal.org/louisiana-prisoners-demand-an-end-to-modern-day-slavery/.

[8] Young, William Paul. Produced by The Wm. Paul Young Initiative. *The Paul Young Podcast.* 2024.

[9] Warren, Rick. 2002. *The Purpose Driven Life.* Chagrin Falls, Oh: Zondervan.

Ten

They'll Know We are Christians by our Love?!

At this point in the book, you're probably thinking to yourself, "Michelle must be really fun at parties!" A little self-deprecating humor there; I get it: I'm a lot!

I've always brought my intensity and my idealism into my friendships. When I was in elementary school, I often came home griping about what this friend did or that friend said, and my mom regularly reminded me that my sister's and brother's friendships never held such drama. My elementary self was desperate to be understood. She was longing to fit in, so she wouldn't stand out in her physical uniqueness. Looking back on that elementary girl, I just want to wrap my arms around her, tell her that her intensity mattered, and help her come up with ways to work through big emotions.

I was generally well-liked; no peer ever bullied me for my physical uniqueness. I am still astonished that any bullying I received was from teachers. I remember an incident in fourth-grade gym class where the teacher yelled at me for a long time, and I had no idea what I had done to make her so angry. Looking back now, I know the teacher was not in a good place, and when I saw her years later, I saw that life had still not been good to her. As a fourth grader, though, I was bewildered and overwhelmed. I didn't care what her life had done to her; I just wanted her to stop yelling at me. A friend's mom worked in the school kitchen, heard the whole fiasco, and felt awful for me. After we got back to class, we had a whole-class discussion about what happened because the other kids were angry. Even though adults seemed capricious, I was thankful that my peers could empathize with me.

****

I continued to have solid friendships throughout my school years. I found that I did better in larger groups or one-on-one. Like the saying goes, "Two's company, three's a crowd." I was listening to a podcast episode the other day where one host talked about her elementary-aged daughter inviting a friend over after a soccer game.[1] The mom wondered why another girl wasn't invited since the three of them typically played so well together. Her daughter's response showed a lot of self-awareness: "I'm worried that the two of them will play, and I'll be left out."

I felt that response deep in my soul because that was my typical experience as well, and it still has an impact on my hangout structure. If it's not a group event, I tend not to invite more than one person at a time because there's still that fear that I won't be included in the conversation. Believe me, it has happened before. The story I heard had a happy ending, and I wish the adults in my life had had the conflict resolution skills that these adults did. The podcast host held a meeting with the three girls and the two other moms, and they hashed out the situation. After the meeting, the host said the girls' conversation was beautiful. She kept hearing, "Is this OK? How are you feeling about...?" And these are elementary-aged kids!

****

Growing up, my house tended to be a hub for my sister's and brother's friends, and I think my parents loved that. They felt thankful to be trusted and got the added bonus of knowing where their own kids were. When I came of age to run around, you could hear the metaphorical *crickets* in our house, and I think that worried my mom especially. She reached out to me in her own way, and I pushed back. Years later, my sister and I had a discussion that was eye-opening for me; though we are both introverted, she tended to get energized by evening hang out sessions, and I got energized by school interactions. By 8:30 pm, which is when I typically left work, I was completely tapped out and had no desire or energy to talk to anyone. Weekends were filled with more homework and work, which also resulted in zero energy. I felt much more understood after she and I had that conversation.

There was a period of time throughout the 2010s where I had multiple jobs, and I learned that I loved networking: "Oh, you want to do 'xyz?' I know someone!' I was able to help people make awesome connections through my vast number of contacts. I worked in a grocery store at one point, and there was one day when I knew at least 25% of my customers; it was amazing. The other cashiers joked that I was socializing on company time!

This networking talent resulted in a big guest list for our wedding, and we heard of multiple interactions that took place: "How do YOU know Keith and Michelle?" Back then, I could have been accused of having only superficial relationships, but I can honestly say that I felt some depth of relationship with each person at the wedding. Each guest was there for a reason.

****

Friendships quieted down a bit after we got married. I consider myself an extroverted introvert, and Keith is 98% introverted, so we don't have many "couple" friends. It's been OK; we've found a system between hanging out and staying in.

In 2018, we embarked on the adventure of changing church homes. We still had good relationships with people, but we felt restless in our current situation. I had changed church homes several times before, and this was Keith's first time. I know people have good intentions when they do this, but it's really not helpful to question why a person leaves a church. Church membership is not equal to a marriage commitment. God moves in different ways, and don't we each need to listen to where He is nudging us? It's not like we're leaving the Body of Christ; we are just moving to a different part. For the person leaving, it is also important to remember that there is no such thing as a perfect church, and if there is, you just ruined it because you're not perfect!

I thought we could check this particular church out because I had been invited to speak at their women's retreat, and we already knew a couple of families who attended. Our eyes were opened to a new world that wasn't Mennonite; this church felt more like a house church and was more informal. Kids ran around before and after the service, most people dressed casually, and the leadership seemed more "grassroots" than "top-down." Mennonite churches tend to be quite structured and desire to have as much order as possible. Some would call that "administration." At this church, there seemed to be a lack of administration, and it felt freeing. At first.

Keith and I felt welcomed, and we started singing on the worship team together. It was actually our first time partnering in a ministry together. Since I love deep talks and coffee shops, I initiated meetups (one-on-one, of course!) and got to know more of the ladies better. The church had been relatively small, but about the time Keith and I started attending, more people started coming.

****

After about a year of attending this church, I noticed a clique starting to form. Before going any further, I should say that my "clique radar" is pretty active, considering I was regularly excluded in youth group growing up. I acknowledge that it could be a simple case of the Baader-Meinhoff Phenomenon: the more a person thinks about something, the more the person sees it in the real world. For example, Lucas and I like pointing out all the Jeeps we see on the road, so since we've been doing that, I've been seeing a lot more Jeeps than I used to. I absolutely admit that this bias could be present in this chapter.

I did my best to put that clique out of my mind and to focus on the people who wanted to socialize with me. At times, it was hard. At outdoor picnics, where "horseshoe" seating arrangements are the norm, inviting others to join, this clique would actually sit in a closed circle just outside of the horseshoe. I was always able to find someone else to talk to, but it was hard to ignore the prick of pain from exclusion. Why was it allowed in plain sight?

Back then, as well as today, I felt the Holy Spirit remind me that cliques aren't healthy. They are, ironically, the result of the fear of being excluded. The people in the cliques go from fearing the monster to becoming the monster. Why would I want to be a part of something that wasn't good for me? Exclusion is never God's plan, so why should I desire to fit in? I understood, but it still bothered me. Why are insecurities allowed to win out without any consequence of accountability?

✳✳✳✳✳✳✳✳✳✳

Lucas eventually arrived, so I gradually forgot about the clique. The church stepped up for a few weeks after Mama's passing, and then everyone faded into the woodwork. I understood that, and I still do. Grief is awkward. Even if someone has lost a loved one, it's still very hard to know how to support someone else whose grief is fresh. Each grief journey is different; some want to talk about it, while others want to act like everything is fine. It's one of those "damned if you do, damned if you don't" situations. I didn't take the lack of support personally because I didn't really know what support I could have used anyway!

I remember one memorable church service in the summer of 2020. It was close to the first anniversary of Mama's accident, and I heard a new voice in the crowd during the worship time. It was strong and boisterous, and when several people gave their testimonies, the voice shouted, "Come on!" I turned to look at one point, and I couldn't see her very well, but I knew she was from the Land of Transformation. My first thought was, "I need a hug from a woman like this!"

As it turns out, she was the speaker for the evening. It was as if Mama had come back and was speaking to me! This woman had the same passionate personality, the same fiery devotion to God, the same fervent prayer life, the same crazy God stories. It was all there. I was close to tears the whole time.

Then she had us listen to a song and invited people to come forward if they wanted to. I did, partly because I wanted to know what the Holy Spirit was saying, but mostly because this woman was so much like Mama, and I desperately wanted to be near her. As the song played, she prayed out loud several times, and at one point, she prayed about running the race to receive the prize. That's when I lost it and started bawling because I knew in my heart that is the very message Mama would want me to hear.

After the song ended, she and her team received prophetic messages for different people in the room, and I sat there, a wet mess, silently pleading with God to give them a word for me. She did come up to me then, saying, "You're going through a lot, aren't you?" I said, "Yes!" I proceeded to tell her a bit about Mama and asked for a hug, which made me start crying all over again. She spent some time encouraging me, telling me to laugh, urging me to move forward, and reassuring me that God is my defender. She even referred to Him as "King of Glory" which was Mama's favorite name for God.

I began to feel people start coming out of the woodwork, excited for me that I had this experience. They hadn't known what to do with my journey in the valley, but they were always available for a party on the mountaintop! Again, I didn't hold anything against them, but I realize now that their behavior was foreshadowing the future.

****

Let's revisit the moment where Lucas' surgery was canceled, and I felt something snap in me in December 2020. The hospital didn't tell us to quarantine until his rescheduled surgery in February, but I didn't know what else to do. I felt like everything else in life had to be paused until my baby got what he needed. I still wanted community, though. I was thankful that our church had online meetings for those who couldn't attend services; it was nice to connect with people that way. I was alarmed, however, when one pastor said, "It's up to the person who stepped away to maintain contact with the church." I didn't want to start an argument, so I kept listening in shocked silence, but I really wanted to ask, "So, people who step away because they have Stage 4 cancer, are solely responsible for their level of contact with the church?!" At that point, I began to notice red flags about this church. I call this incident "Red Flag #1."

Perhaps Red Flag #1 was so alarming for me because in some of my relationships, I am the force that keeps it going. I keep the relationships going because I know my friends don't mean anything by their lack of checking in. Life is busy; I get it, and I love them dearly. Our times together are always amazing, and I believe they're worth my effort to reach out. However, I've had the thought numerous times over the years, "If I didn't reach out, would my social life disappear?" After hearing what the pastor said, I realized, "I guess so!"

I continued reaching out and included people from the church. One friend from the church regularly talked to me on the phone, which was really sweet because she hates phone calls. She put her discomfort aside for me, and our chats were such a gift. I talked to another person from church a few times, but otherwise, people didn't take time for me, even when I asked to connect. I made it clear that I didn't need to vent or be "ministered to"; I just wanted to hear about life outside of my house. What were people up to? Who did something silly, crazy, or meaningful? There was a lot of silence. Red flag #2.

Around that time, I thought of a memory from my first trip to The Land of Transformation. The two leaders of the team were best buds and formed a little clique of their own. There were a bunch of giggly college-aged girls and a woman in her 40s. I was 25 and felt like a loner. At the end of the trip, we each had an individual debriefing time with the leaders, and I said my only criticism was that I wished for more connecting time with the leaders. Just a quick 5-minute check-in to see how I was every day. I was sick for several days on that trip, and no one cared enough to act, other than Mama. Their response was, "Oh! We thought you were good; you seemed very strong and capable, so we just let you do your own thing."

What that distant memory from 2012 revealed about me in 2021 is that I wasn't needy; I didn't need obvious help or support, and I also wasn't in the "in-group." I was in no man's land. In the church, there was a family in the clique who quarantined for three weeks, and the church sent them care packages. We quarantined for two months and got nothing. Remember how I said I enjoyed the lack of administrative skills in the church at first? Well, this was an example of where the administrative lack was blatantly obvious. I know there weren't malicious intentions; I know they were busy. But this whole scenario confirmed that the "seemingly strong" people don't need help. They're able to fend for themselves and are left to their own devices. Red Flag #3.

****

Lucas' second surgery was successful and other than a brief repair surgery later in 2021, he hasn't needed anything since. Our check-ups at the hospital are spaced out every two years now, which feels incredible; we have finally been able to put that stage behind us.

We started back to church right after the surgery, just in time for "Child Dedication," which is different from baptism; it's more of a declaration that parents make that they will raise their children in a way that honors Jesus. The dedication service felt like a good reentry into the group, and I felt the anxiety and despair slip away. Interestingly enough, the message during that service was about including others, and the pastor said in all the places he has lived, my area has been the most exclusive and "clique-filled" area. He said his wife, who is from the area, is probably the main reason he made any friends and connections at all. I was pleasantly surprised and encouraged by the message.

A few days later, I got a message from one of the people in the clique; she asked if I wanted to get together. I was pretty shocked, but I agreed. We had a good conversation, and I was honest about some of the things I had experienced. I didn't bring up the clique factor, but otherwise, she was sympathetic and wished that my experience could have been different. We ended the evening with an invitation from her to join a workout night; most of the clique would be there, but there would be others as well. I was optimistic about a fresh start, so I agreed.

This was the beginning of the end of my time in this church.

****

The workout experience made me feel like I was in middle school again. While some people talked to me, others had pretty poor social skills. I need to look at it that way to have any kind of empathy for them because these people clearly weren't in a good place. When I started talking to one woman, she abruptly turned and began a conversation with someone else. Another woman saw me heading toward her - we made eye contact - and she walked away.

Did I really forfeit an evening with Keith and Lucas for this? To try to fit in with a group that would obviously never accept me for who I am? That evening was a turning point for me, and I knew I had to talk to someone at the church about the situation. I didn't want to go to the men in the pastoral team, because I could just imagine the eye rolls thinking about "girl drama," so I went to three of their wives. Over my years there, I felt like I could trust them. I felt like we could have a healthy "back and forth" about all this.

I sent the three of them a voice message via the Marco Polo app and made myself vulnerable. I want to be clear that my goal was never to say, "Make them be friends with me." It's impossible to force friendships. Author Glennon Doyle talks about an image of a home that fits my goal well. She talks about different spheres of relationships; there's the "front yard" sphere where everyone should be welcome. There's the "foyer" sphere where a person can go beyond small talk to a point. Then there's the "dinner table" sphere, which symbolizes one of the most intimate spots in a home where people can share everything.

My goal was the "front yard" sphere. The church was small enough that the clique was obvious. Was I naive enough to think that the church should have a "front yard" atmosphere? I wanted to brainstorm ways to make the atmosphere more "front-yard" friendly. I came up with at least one suggestion that they thought was great, but nothing ever came of it. It felt like a blatant lack of administration to me. We scheduled a time to meet in a few months to talk more in-depth.

In the meantime, women in the church were conducting a book study, and we met about a week or so after the workout experience. At one point, out of curiosity, I steered the conversation towards the concept of accountability. I asked a question to the effect of, "If someone comes to you and says you did 'xyz' and your actions really hurt them, how would you respond?" The answers ranged from what I expected, "Well, I'm not perfect, so they need to understand that," to the alarmingly bizarre, "I only like it when God confronts me." No one suggested humility. That conversation was chilling, and it foreshadowed what was to come.

****

Around this time, members of the leadership team started telling the church, "It's great to hear what God has done in your life, but we also want to hear from you in the middle of the storm. What is He teaching you in the hard times?" I wanted to scream "Lies!" at the top of my lungs because I hadn't been experiencing fellowship; I experienced awkward silences, if not mild shunning.

In March of 2021, I finally went public with how I was feeling on social media. I wrote the following:

'Yesterday, I learned that a Christian singer moved on from Christianity. It was a bombshell because her music has blessed me so much. It's why I'm up at 3 am writing this post.

I don't really know any of the details...but the even bigger bombshell to me is: I don't blame her one bit. Now, please hear me out. I love Jesus, and I will always follow Him. In the words of Peter, "Where else would I go?"

I'm saying with regards to the Church - the Bride of Christ, not one specific group of people - I don't blame her and others for leaving. I'd imagine the Church is a big reason for her leaving, because once you know Jesus, could He ever be a reason for you to walk away?

I have really been struggling with finding love for the Church over this past half year in particular. I have to remind myself that I'm part of the Church, and the only one I can control is myself. My time of grief - coupled with everything COVID - has shown me where I've fallen short as a sister and how I need to do better.

I no longer put people on pedestals.
I no longer desire to be on a pedestal.

I no longer desire to be exclusive.
I no longer desire to be part of something exclusive.

I desire to be in community with people who openly admit they struggle.

I desire to be in community with people who don't have all the answers.

I desire to be in community with people who admit it when they're wrong and who help me do the same!

I desire to be in community with people who want to learn from each other, to ask deep questions, and to encourage one another.

I desire to be in community with people who aren't afraid to show up to awkward situations and stay as long as they need to.

I desire to be in community with people who go after the one lost sheep. The lost sheep are not non-believers. The lost sheep are the people who have moved on from the faith because they have been scared away.'

It took me almost two hours to write and edit that post, and the whole time, I asked God if this was a good idea. Whether or not I heard Him correctly, it's probably easy to imagine that people didn't appreciate my post.

****

The meeting with the three women on the church leadership team took place one afternoon in April, and about an hour before the meeting, I had a strong instinct that it wasn't going to go well. The meeting started off as I expected, with the ladies urging me to examine how I need to change my way of thinking and to empathize with members of the clique. I've since come to learn that that is classic victim-shaming and deflection.

About halfway through the meeting, the three ladies all looked at each other briefly, paused, and launched into the fact that my social media posts were most likely the cause of division and disunity. I felt blindsided because again, I wasn't trying to get the group to like me. I was trying to make the church services more "front-yard" friendly. Suddenly, I'm the sole cause of the problem? I'm not claiming innocence here, by any stretch of the imagination, but this was quite the jump.

I didn't know how to proceed with that church anymore. Did everyone truly think I was the problem? Throughout the following year, my attendance was pretty sporadic at the church; I was fine if Keith went, but I didn't want to go anymore. In the spring of 2022, Keith wanted to give a message to the church about something un-related, and met with the lead pastor several times in preparation. A few months later, when Keith was frustrated with my lack of church attendance, he shared that the lead pastor said to him, "Michelle is re-ally confusing. We've been meeting to try to figure out how to please her, but nothing has worked."

RECORD SCRATCH...

They've had meetings ABOUT me...WITHOUT ME?! That was the last straw, and I was officially done with that group.

****

I saw a post from a person on social media who owns sheep, and he talked about a fatal mistake that he made. He left a sheepdog in charge who wasn't quite mature enough to be left alone with the sheep. Sure, the sheepdog had training, but at this particular moment, he wanted to mess with the sheep. This mischief caused absolute chaos, and when the man went out to see what was going on, he noticed there was a dead sheep. Alarmed, he counted the rest of the sheep and re-alized a ewe was missing. After looking for a considerable amount of time, he found her hiding and shaking in terror.

He related this event to the Church at large. He said that when someone leaves a congregation - or the Church as a whole - we often blame that person. We say it's because the person was living in some kind of sin and didn't want to repent, or we say the person didn't reach out enough. How was the church even supposed to know the person was struggling?

The man said flat out that the dead sheep and the terrified ewe were his fault. The sheepdog will be a good sheepdog in time, but he should have known that the dog wasn't quite ready to be on his own. Are the pastors in any given church mature enough and ready enough to pastor their own flock? He ended his post with the question, "What if people didn't leave the church on their own? What if they were driven away?"

This post resonated with me deeply and made me ache to see more humility in the Church.

****

For a while, Lucas watched the *Toy Story* movies regularly, and I was surprised how one scene in the third movie often choked me up[2]. The main toys trusted one toy who ended up being the villain. At the end of the movie, they all, including the villain, found themselves heading to the incinerator, so they worked together to try to save themselves. The villain found his way to safety and also had a way to save the others. The others cried out to him for help, and he ran away laughing. The others were eventually saved, but it's a harrowing minute or so until then.

I think I choked up because ever since the fiasco with the ministry to help others in The Land of Transformation, betrayal has been my experience with so many people. I've stepped out in faith, believing that people truly had great intentions with me, only to step back after the fact and look at the wreckage in disbelief, wondering where I went wrong. Is my "people radar" broken?

One thing is for sure as I mentioned in Chapter 1. I love expectations and form a lot of them, either knowingly or unknowingly. I've heard a lot of quotes about expectations, and one of my favorites is something along the lines of, "Expectations are resentments under construction." My issue may simply be that I expect too much from people because I expect too much from myself.

Finally, I found myself getting somewhere in all of this drama, because I can only change myself, after all. This "expectation" piece is something I can work on.

****

When someone is going through a dark time, it's common for people to say that the sun will shine again. It's true. The darkness doesn't last forever, but that cliche has always felt lacking to me somehow.

I read somewhere on social media that essentially said[3] "Yes, the sun will rise again. But the landscape the sun rises on may look entirely different from the landscape that the sun set on."

That's it! That's why the statement has felt empty all this time. Yes, a new day will come, but you may be surrounded by devastation and destruction. At least, it may look that way. The sun may rise on an entirely new way of life for you, and that's rarely easy.

What I saw heading into 2022 was that my family was still intact. Keith and Lucas will always be my most important earthly relationships. But looking around, I saw heaps of ashes everywhere. Was anything else salvageable? Over the past few years, I'd been walking around, checking the structural integrity of places I'd been and people with whom I'd been trying to engage. Some things have held and remained solid while others have crumbled at the touch.

Some days, it's really hard to believe that God is a God of restoration. It's hard to hope that God can make things new, that He is doing a new thing. It's hard to trust that God works everything for my good. It's hard to stop clinging to the lie that I'm alone and that I am responsible for everything.

It's hard, but it's not impossible.

Around the beginning of 2022, a friend and I were reading *The Broken Way* by Ann Voskamp[4]. It's a fantastic book, and I'd read it several times before. She talks about how the soil has to break before seeds can be planted, and a seed has to die before it can bring forth the crop. Life comes from the breaking of something. She says, "If you don't know what life is supposed to look like, you might think it is complete destruction."

2022 was about to bring the greatest appearance of destruction yet, and I just want to hug the Chapter 10 version of me because she had no idea how much more she had to endure.

NOTES

[1] Doyle, Glennon, et al. Produced by Allison Schott, et al. *We Can Do Hard Things.* 2025.

[2] Unkrich, Lee , dir. 2010. *Toy Story 3.* Film. Pixar.

[3] Benfield, Jillian . 2022. Review of *The Sun Will Come out Again. Jillian Benfield* (Facebook). February 17, 2022. https://tinyurl.com/3cr2hfvt.

[4} Voskamp, Ann. 2016. *The Broken Way : A Daring Path to the Abundant Life.* Grand Rapids, Michigan: Zondervan.

Eleven

In Sickness and Health?

In seventh grade, my English teacher asked the class what age we were most looking forward to. For some unknown reason, I said "27." I know that I liked the number 7, and I must have liked the number 2, as well. Everyone was saying 16, 18, 21, and as soon as I blurted out "27," I was embarrassed because even the teacher had a quizzical look on her face.

Looking back, saying "27" actually makes a little more sense now. Remember when I was busy with plans to spend the summer in The Land of Transformation and was up to my neck in grad school work and jobs? Even though life was incredibly hectic, I remember feeling so ALIVE, so "in the zone," so confident of what my future was going to hold. I was 27. The Pursuit Challenge I mentioned was in my 27th year, and it transformed me. I was truly content with how life was unfolding, and I wouldn't change a thing about my 27th year.

As I'm thinking about what this chapter holds, I am so grateful for how content I was at 27. When Keith asked me out, I couldn't even fathom being in a relationship at first. I am so thankful for my awareness of the gift of being the perfect companion to myself all this time. To be truly comfortable in my own skin and to deal with my issues down to the deepest layer that I could as a single person is something I have not taken for granted as a married person. That is not to say

I was perfect, because I absolutely wasn't. I just felt intentional, goal-oriented, and purposeful.

Even as we were dating and engaged, Keith and I took our time and spent almost two years getting to know each other, seeing how our lives would fit together. It didn't scare us that we got married at almost 30; I actually love that our wedding ushered in the next decade of life for both of us. Our 20s were a time of separate and individual growth, a time that both of us used intentionally to let the Holy Spirit guide us and mold us into who we are today. The two pastors who were a part of our wedding ceremony each affirmed our relationship before the wedding, with one of them saying, "When I look at the two of you, I just feel peace."

****

While living out the content of this chapter in real time, I clung desperately to everything mentioned in the last section. These memories were a reminder that making the right decisions could actually be easy when what I'd been walking out was the exact opposite - right decisions are often extremely hard to make.

Before diving into the depths of this chapter, I want to make two things clear:

1. This was no one's fault.
2. This happened **to** us. Not because of any poor decision but simply because life just throws hard times at us, as the previous chapters have also made clear.

****

One thing I love about my relationship with Keith is that we are on the same page about 90% of life. Holy Spirit, finances, and child rearing - that alignment has made a lot of our marriage journey relatively easy. A partnership like that is wonderful.

However, in 2021, I started to notice a slight shift. I reasoned to myself that the intensity of our life, the impact of COVID, as well as the 2020 election results/insurrection at the Capitol, have taken a toll on all of us. These events led to some highly intense discussions in 2021. It was often so hard to even imagine that we could reconcile our differences in those areas. Also, we decided to move that spring, so that made things much more stressful.

The thing is, convictions on issues like politics and world events aren't easy to reconcile. Some things we never will see eye-to-eye on, and maybe we're not supposed to. There is beauty in difference and diversity; after all, God doesn't download all of His revelations into one type of person. We need each other. I've often thought about something a friend told us when we were engaged - we need a healthy amount of tension for things to run effectively. He gave several examples of things that have too much or too little tension (which I don't remember), and they don't work without the necessary amount of tension.

I noticed the tension shifts in little things -

-Keith used to be adventurous with me in the kitchen. He soon became more rigid, wondering why we had to try complicated new recipes.

-As we were reading a book together, we came across a word neither of us had seen before. While I, who holds a Master's Degree, was perfectly fine looking up the definition, Keith was frustrated that the author hadn't chosen a more accessible word.

-Keith began to experience a strange sensation in his arm in the middle of the night, at the same time of night, for months. I urged him to go to the doctor, and he didn't believe it was a symptom of anything physical. I wanted to be an empathetic wife, but at 1:30 am, I had nothing to offer but a quick prayer to make it all stop, for the love of God, because the two of us desperately needed sleep. We would learn later that this sensation was called a sensory hallucination.

****

These shifts in tension happened during the church fiasco from Chapter 10, and I found myself looking for support that wasn't there. Don't get me wrong; I wasn't expecting that Keith would be 100% in agreement with me. I wanted maybe 50% of agreement with an empathetic ear for the rest. It didn't come. What came instead were abrupt responses and strange accusations that left me feeling defiant and thinking, "I'm not submitting to shame."

I didn't really know who else to talk to about these shifts in tension, as the default answer in some of my circles is, "Stop overthinking things; you're fine. You're too sensitive, and it's nothing." I do remember a pastor friend sensing the dynamic between us and calling it out. He offered to meet with us on a more regular basis, which we accepted because we always enjoyed gleaning from his insights.

Those meetings didn't have much of an effect on our relationship. The insights were great, but when it came to talking about things, Keith didn't say much. I'm an open book, so I shared freely and realized that the one who shares freely is the one who receives most of the corrective feedback. I say this without judgment because this friend corrects with the best balance of truth and grace I have ever experienced. I didn't fault him, and I didn't fault Keith; I just felt more and more like something was off, and I didn't know the first thing about fixing it.

****

There was no improvement or further decline throughout the last months of 2021 into 2022. I felt cautiously optimistic at the beginning of 2022 and got connected to a nutritionist to start healthier physical habits. I began to feel better and started allowing myself to feel hope.

Around April, the positive feelings began to fade again. I cried a lot that month. It may have been what I was going through at the time, but I think it might have been catch-up from the previous years when the tears just wouldn't come. One thing that did happen left me reeling for a while.

I got berated for something I didn't do, and the adult did it in front of students. The students were gracious, and they made up for it. One student played a recording of something he composed on the piano himself. A 6th grader composing a 4-minute piece on the piano! It was beautiful and so soothing.

I was reeling because I didn't understand why the event happened. Then it came to me - I'm not afraid to be vulnerable; I honestly have no choice. It comes as naturally to me as breathing, and that scares the shit out of some adults. As a result, they either attack it or exploit it to their own gain. It's exhausting. Maybe that's why kids always make it better. They're vulnerable, too, and we're affirming each other in it.

****

Personal and professional stuff kept building through May. I wrote about this particular experience on social media:

At the grocery store today, I didn't help an older lady in a motorized cart.

I saw her as I turned down an aisle. "Excuse me?" she asked politely. The words came automatically, "I don't work here," as I hustled past. She didn't receive that well, yelling at me from her spot in the aisle. I said nothing more. I saw her later in another aisle where she picked up her tirade from where she had left off. I still said nothing more.

I was honestly surprised that I had responded to her that way, yet after processing the experience, I am OK with how I handled it.

Admittedly, having worked in retail before, ladies in motorized carts don't bring up fond memories. Perhaps my response originated there.

But also....

Maybe I would have had the energy to help her if I hadn't been berated by a parent earlier this week for not being perfect.

Maybe I would have had the energy to help if it wasn't that time of year to respond to the slew of emails wondering why students are failing.

Maybe I would have had the energy to help if I could unlock the mystery that is my toddler's eating habits.

I'm tired. I have compassion fatigue from being urged to take on responsibility that isn't mine. I spend so much energy on Lucas (who is my full responsibility, of course!) and my students (who try to push their responsibility on me) these days that I don't have a lot to give anyone else anymore. When Mama died almost three years ago, I lost my reserve emotional energy tank, and to this day, I don't know if I have ever been at a full tank of original emotional energy.

Consider this post an invitation not to put out every fire you are asked to - even if it is something as simple as helping someone in the grocery store. Other people's urgency is not your emergency. Your capacity to help will vary from day to day, and that's OK. Also, extend the grace to other people when they decline your request for help. Their capacity may already be met for the day.

I realize this all flies in the face of JOY - Jesus, Others, Yourself. I've never been a fan of that anyway, though. With it being Mental Health Awareness month, may I challenge you to take care of yourself, too? As someone once said, "It's not 'me first,' it's 'me, too.'"

****

I find it interesting that I wrote that post during Mental Health Awareness Month because the issues Keith and I were walking through stemmed from his mental health, though neither of us was aware of it at the time. Keep in mind what I wrote earlier in this chapter - neither of us was at fault, and this happened **to** us.

Starting in June, Keith began experiencing another concerning trait - finding threats in places I couldn't see. I had to switch roles with him at that point; I had to be the rational voice to his irrational thoughts, and this was not a role I felt equipped to play. I was able to stay calm, though, and we kept stumbling our way through "whatever this was."

In August, this "threat-finding" amped up to a whole new level. In his desire to protect me, Lucas, and himself, Keith accused a friend of doing something that this friend didn't do. It was devastating, and I knew something had to change. I just didn't know what. We did agree to see a more experienced counselor, and while that was a bit of a help, I still felt like I had to white knuckle my way through life, feeling alone, confused, sad, and angry.

****

In the last week of August, the situation took a nosedive. Keith didn't get much sleep, and his symptoms escalated. One night, I was in the bathroom with the lights off; I like to preserve my "sleepiness" that way. I didn't realize that Keith was awake until I was bathed in light. "What are you doing?!" I mumbled angrily. Then I looked up and knew things weren't OK. He wasn't mentally present for a few seconds, and his eyes were frantic. After a bit, he turned the lights off and went back to the kitchen. I followed him, tried to stay calm and to reason with him, but I just couldn't get through to him.

The next day dawned to more weirdness, and this time, family members actually asked me if things were OK. I was honest with them and told them everything. Later that day, I did something I don't often do; I prayed in tongues. In a nutshell, this is how I would define the practice: I know I don't have human words for this situation, and in the book of Romans, it talks about how the Spirit intercedes for us when we don't have the words. These utterings look different for different people; each person can have their own prayer language. I don't believe it's a foundational issue, so if you don't pray in tongues, yet you still follow Jesus, that's totally fine.

I compare the experience of praying in tongues to exercise - at the start, it feels laborious, but in the end, I feel better. As I was praying in tongues that morning, I felt the Holy Spirit plead to me in a way I hadn't heard before. "Please keep going with Keith. He is still there, but the Keith you see in front of you is an imposter. Please don't give up. It will be worth it in the end."

Keith didn't come home from work at the normal time that day and didn't answer my calls. When he finally got home, I said, "We need to talk. Something needs to change." He said OK and then went to take a shower. After he finished, he was extremely antsy and couldn't stop moving around. He kept saying that he couldn't stay at our house; he needed to go somewhere else. I had to get right in his face to stop him from moving and demanded to know what was going on: "Why can't you stay here?" He replied, "Because I am afraid that I will hurt you and Lucas."

****

Some people tend to perform best under stress; that's why we have ER doctors and the medical field in general. I...don't. I've always hated the thought of being the responsible one in an emergency. I tend to freeze and even dissociate in some stressful situations. In this moment, however, I became extremely calm and my mind was crystal clear. It was obviously God. "You need to go to the psychiatric ward," I calmly stated. He agreed right away, which surprised me. Later on, he shared that the overwhelm he felt was too great to make any decisions, so he was relieved when I made the decision. Again, none of this was his fault. This was happening **to** him.

I was glad that our local hospital wasn't too far away because I didn't know what the car ride there would be like. What if he grabbed the wheel as I was driving? Would he be OK with Lucas in the backseat? In the end, he sat up front with me and seemed more level-headed, almost relieved that there was a solution to the way he was feeling. Before he got out of the car at the hospital, we prayed together, and I told him I was proud of him for admitting he needed help.

Then Lucas and I headed to my parents' house, where I was finally able to hide and let the tears flow. Lucas didn't seem fazed by the evening's events; it was one of the many times I've been thankful for technology's distraction. I made some calls, and people agreed to pray.

I barely slept that night, and the next morning, I asked my dad to come back to our house with me. I had heard somewhere that behavioral health hospitals wouldn't discharge patients while there were firearms in the house, so I wanted my dad to take the firearms out of our house. It was a sobering experience, yet slightly validating because now people were seeing what I'd been seeing all along - things weren't OK, and we needed some kind of intervention.

I didn't know if I should call the hospital or if I should wait for Keith to call. I communicated with his work, and they were willing to accommodate our situation. Late that morning, a friend texted:

-How's Keith doing? Do you know which place they are taking him to?

Me: I don't know. I'm waiting for someone to call.

Friend: You should call and find out where he is.

That encouragement spurred me into action, and I called our local hospital. Thankfully, Keith had had the presence of mind to put my name down as an emergency contact, so the person could give me information. He had been transferred to a new location about an hour before I called, and his stay at the hospital had been relatively uneventful...except for when it wasn't. Essentially, in his desire to be protective of others, he revealed that his true need was to be protected himself. He later told me he was so glad that the incident didn't happen at home.

****

That day, I was so thankful for the support from others. I had an emergency session with my spiritual director, and I was able to be with friends around whom I could truly fall apart. I had three phones on me that I kept looking at constantly - my phone, Keith's personal phone, and his work phone. I had a mini meltdown when I found out that Keith called his mom before he called me, but a friend shed some light on the situation. She had also spent time at a behavioral health hospital, and the only phone number that she could remember was her childhood home number. It turns out that was the case with Keith.

Later, I saw an unknown number pop up on one of the phones, but by the time I realized it was probably Keith, the phone stopped ringing. I tried calling the number and had another meltdown when the call didn't go through. Another friend explained to me that in situations like this, the patients can call out, but we aren't able to call in.

Later that night, I had an online session with our joint counselor, and he told me, "Michelle, what you both are going through is not due to marriage issues. It's due to Keith's mental health, and neither of you is at fault." I just started sobbing, finally relieved to be free of the burden that all of this was something I had to fix.

During the meeting with our counselor, I got a call from Keith on his work phone. I quickly said goodbye to the counselor, and with my hands shaking from nerves, I picked up the phone. I was so thankful to hear his voice, and all things considered, he sounded OK. He said for the first day, the protocol was for him to be in his own room, and he said the nurses let him be when he asked for some space. He received some blood tests because his symptoms can sometimes be a result of physical issues. He said he was really tired and that he was going to get some sleeping aids that night. He expressed regret for not admitting he needed help sooner, and I reminded him that admitting he needed help was better later rather than never. Sometimes we need to hit rock bottom before things can begin to improve. I assured him that I was proud of him for getting healthy for himself, for me, and for Lucas. I then asked if he felt that he was being treated with kindness and dignity. He said everyone was very kind to him.

****

I asked that question every time we talked because there is such a stigma to mental health. Sometimes people might view those who suffer from mental health conditions as monsters who can't be redeemed - even the people who work with this population can have that opinion. Sometimes in the Church, people are urged to focus solely on their spiritual health, and that is dangerous because we are spiritual, physical, and mental beings. I believe there is a spiritual component for sure, but it is foolish to act as if that's the only factor.

This stigma is also a reason that I am hesitant to write this chapter because people's discomfort with the unknown often leads to callous explanations and advice. Of course, the people have good intentions, but the hidden fear they aren't discussing is that "There needs to be a logical formulaic reason it happened to them, so I can assure myself it won't happen to me." That's another example of hubris - a dangerous overconfidence that your life will go the way you expect as long as you do the right things. Keith and I confidently said "in sickness and in health" in our wedding vows, fully expecting sickness to show up in our 70s and 80s – not at 35. We had zero clue that our lives would include this journey. In fact, if someone had said, "One of you will spend time in a behavioral health hospital," both of us would have immediately guessed that it would be me, not Keith.

I just wanted to be sure that he was treated like a human being, not just some obstacle someone needed to overcome to get through a work day. Every day, he confirmed that they were being kind and supportive with whatever needs he had at the time. I was also happy to hear that the food was good, because you just never know.

There wasn't much on the daily schedule for Keith to do at the hospital. Remember how I said Keith was so overwhelmed the night I dropped him off at the hospital? Brene Brown notes in her book *Atlas of the Heart*[1] that the only cure for overwhelm is to do nothing. That is the structure of behavioral health hospitals - to give the brain plenty of space and time to rest. Keith was BORED. He had group therapy and some other planned activities, but he mostly had time to think, to pray, to wonder, and dream about what the future would look like. He regularly asked me to pray that his time in the hospital would accomplish something. I told him that it already was - by getting healthy himself, he was working at keeping our family healthy. We got to talk at least twice a day - once on the phone and once on FaceTime. They didn't allow in-person visits due to COVID, but hey, that saved on gas, at least!

****

As I mentioned before, I stopped going to church in the spring of 2022. Whenever people leave church, others well-intentionally try to guilt-trip them by saying, "Well, who's going to support you in a crisis if you don't have a church family?" The late author Rachel Held Evans once thought to herself as she left her church for the last time, "If I ever have a baby, who's going to bring me a meal?"[2] I get it; it's one of the elements of community that is glaringly obvious when it's absent.

During the three weeks that Keith was in the hospital, though, my true community made itself known, and it was made up of people who had been in my life for years and years. They helped by babysitting Lucas, by inviting me for meals, by dropping meals off, by sending texts, and by calling. I remember one day when I got a notification that Keith sold something on Ebay. I've never sold anything on Ebay, and with all that was going on, even something this insignificant sent me over the edge. Thankfully, I remembered a friend who sells things on Ebay, and she was able to walk me through the process of canceling the order. That "little" gesture saved my sanity for one more day. Keith's work also sent us a paycheck each week for the amount of 40 hours' worth of work, which was extremely generous.

In times of crisis, people also learn who is not in their corner. I had been texting the pastor of the church from Chapter 10 of Keith's situation - not because I needed something from the church, but because I knew Keith still wanted to be connected with the church. After a few days, though, the pastor stopped responding to my updates, so I simply stopped updating. In Chapter 10, I mentioned that if I'm not in need or if I'm not a part of the "in" group, I'm in "no man's" land, but this experience proved me wrong. My family was in crisis mode, and we were still ignored. I wanted to say I couldn't care less about that group, but in reality, I was pissed that I still felt hurt by that group of people. After all this time, why did I still want to feel like they cared about me? I tried to pray, "Bless them and release me." The main reason God wants us to forgive is so we can be free to live out the rest of our lives the way He intended us to. People are going to do stupid stuff - myself included - so it is vital that we muster up the strength and the humility to move on to better things and release the past to the only One who can redeem it.

****

I missed Mama so much over this period. I know she would have shared cliches, but coming from her, they never seemed like empty words because she walked them out daily. With her, cliches were more like examples, as though she were saying, "Follow me!" I know she would have been praying fervently for our situation, too. She would have made herself available to me as often as she could, and she would have tried to get on a call with Keith, too, to encourage him and pray with him personally. She was never afraid to go deep in the hard places of life, and I ached for that.

I was trying to be strong for Lucas, and to let some of my steam out, but my road rage increased! It was never more than horn-blowing, but I did it with gusto. At least one time, Lucas asked if I was mad, and I was honest with him. I told him that Daddy was sick, and he's at the hospital getting better. Talking about this road rage makes me think of the incident in the grocery store from earlier in this chapter. I realize that when I am in a good place, I can help people with insignificant tasks and can be patient with other drivers. When I'm not in a good place, though, those emotions are going to spill out somewhere, and I have decided that "somewhere" will be strangers. Ideally, it's no one specifically, but if I lose my cool, I would rather lose it on people I probably won't see again than those I love most in the world. How many stories have we all heard about people coming home after a stressful day and taking it out on their loved ones who were guilty only of being in "the wrong place at the wrong time?" I don't want to be like that. I want to be kind to everyone, but in the moments where I feel like I have to choose, I want my little family to be the recipient of kindness. It's like being between a rock and a hard place.

****

While Keith was in the hospital, I had the rare experience of being validated for my feelings. Keith's case worker was amazing, and she took notes on what I shared with her. I was intimidated when she told me that Keith wouldn't be discharged until I was ready. How was I supposed to know that? I soon realized that once Keith felt good about staying on medication, that was the reassurance I needed. Because he admitted himself to the hospital, he had the option to leave three days before the recommended date of discharge. He ended up staying until the recommended date, and that felt good to me. I reminded him that none of this is a race, that the only person he should compete with is the person he was yesterday. I told him again and again how proud I was of him and of the ways he was breaking chains from his past. His quiet defiance in the face of despair inspires me to this day.

I just have one more note on the importance of validation. Recently, a friend said something so simple yet so profound. She said, "Michelle, when Keith said he was afraid he would hurt you and Lucas, you believed him. Do you know what an incredible gift that was for him? If he had said that to someone else, and that person had brushed him off, think of what could have happened." Essentially, her comment showed me that validation can alter the course of people's lives. Whoa!

****

His homecoming ushered in a period of time where we moved at the speed of turtle. We had to learn a new normal, and I was on high alert for anything that seemed amiss. Thankfully, Keith was matched to a psychiatrist and could meet with him two weeks after being discharged from the hospital. That was a miracle because psychiatrists are few and far between. A lot of people need to wait months before being able to see one. We noticed that Lucas had meltdowns that lasted longer than normal, but we were able to empathize with him because he had to process these events, too. There was a happy ending with the friend with whom Keith had a conflict; he and Keith had a good talk, and their previous relationship was restored.

In December, I was able to get away for the weekend to attend a "Dark Night of the Soul" retreat. During my time away, I had permission to lament - we even received a template for writing our own laments - and to wrestle. I had a bit of a breakthrough in the first session already. I hadn't been asking God, "Where are You?" Instead, I'd been asking God, "What GOOD are You?" I'd known all along that God was with me, but I thought at best, He was just standing there with His arms folded, waiting for me to act. At worst, I thought He was shrugging His shoulders, admitting He was powerless to do anything. In realizing my true question, I felt that God was like, "YES. We are FINALLY getting somewhere." While still chewing that over, one of the leaders read this quote:

"This morning, I greet the God who is more God than the god I greet." - Pádraig Ó Tuama

Cue the next step in my revelation. The god of whom I've been asking the question, "What good are you?" isn't the true god. The true

God is bigger than that god, more present than that god, more gracious and compassionate than that god.

We talked a lot about mystery. We talked a lot about finding safety in uncertainty, and we ended the retreat with a poem entitled "Hope is not a Bird, Emily, it's a Sewer Rat" by Caitlin Seida. It's a response to an Emily Dickinson poem and is an irreverent, hilarious, and spot-on interpretation of hope. Look it up!

During that weekend, I noticed something fascinating. As deeply and seriously as we delved into our questions and doubts in the sessions, that's exactly how light and silly our mealtimes were! It drove home a point I had thought of for a while - when I can truly wrestle and be real with someone, that's when I can also truly celebrate with them. Being vulnerable with others unlocks a childlikeness in me that I don't always let other people see.

I closed out 2022 with a defiant and dogged sense of hope.

****

The first half of 2023 was awful, and I'm just going to sum it up in three social media posts from that time period:

1. I'm reading the book *Caste* by Isabel Wilkerson[3], which argues that the US functions via an intricate caste system. I'm learning that I have been in the "physically inferior" caste all my life, and Keith has now entered the "mentally inferior" caste. No wonder I'm so dang tired.

In the Old Testament, it talks a lot about the kings who do right in the eyes of the LORD, except for when they don't remove the high places. At first read, it's just like, "C'mon guys; if it's a high place, it's gotta be pretty easy to see to remove!" Then it hit me: high places are values so ingrained in our culture that we are blind to them. In this day and age of the US, I believe the caste system is one of our high places.

A poem off the top of my head about our personal experiences with caste:

When you've been swimming against the current your whole life
And you're wondering why you can't swim with it.
Only to find out...they never intended to let you swim with them in
the first place.
It's an issue of caste.

When you have to plot out every move you're going to make before you make it, because society doesn't feel the need to be bothered
by your needs.
It's an issue of caste.

When you feel pressured to socialize, because society
doesn't know how to deal with introverts.
It's an issue of caste.

When your worth is determined by what you do rather than who
you are, because
society values dollar signs over health and well-being.
It's an issue of caste.

When you read in the Word of God that we need to care for the alien,
the orphan, and the widow,
and the nationalist, the popular, and the wealthy are prized instead.
It's an issue of caste.

2. There's so much stirring in me right now. I guess I'll start with
something Jesus told me five years ago:

"You're not able to fully grasp the significance of the promise that
the last will be first." "Gee, I wonder why I can't fully grasp it."

Jesus: Oh, hey, these people are hungry. Let's feed them!
The Church today: "If you don't work, you don't eat."

Jesus: "Hey, welcome to the group of disciples, Judas!"
The Church today: "You're too.../not...enough. You can be on the
outer edges, but don't even think about coming in close!"

Jesus: "Let the little children come to Me!"
The Church today: "Let's cram all the kids into a primary department that is extremely understaffed and the people are miserably over-worked."

Jesus: "Let him who is without sin cast the first stone."
The Church today: "GRAB ALL OF THE STONES"

Yes, I'm angry. Yes, I'm frustrated. In case I wasn't yet clear enough. I don't understand why Jesus' plea for us to advocate for those on the fringes has fallen onto complacent ears. I don't understand that the Church today thinks we need to live comfortable lives when Jesus did, in fact, say that we will have troubles. Why are we clamoring to be the priest and the Levite when it's the Samaritan who actually did the right thing?

When Jesus promised that the last will be first, was He inviting us to see life urgently? We only have so much time here, so if we hoard all of this crap, will we be completely empty on the other side? In the parable of the barn builder, the angel comes to tell the man he's going to die that very night, but...not because he had so much money, as we often interpret it to mean.

He was going to die because he didn't share the money. He didn't invest in the lives around him. He didn't meet the needs that were surrounding him. He kept it all for himself. What's the use of a life if you keep everything all for yourself? Ann Voskamp talks about cancer in her book *The Broken Way*; she says, normally, cells die so new ones can come to continue the cycle of life. Cancer cells don't die; they just keep coming and head the body towards destruction.

I thank God for that promise that the last will be first. I'm thankful that in the midst of all this chaos, He's here in the mystery, making something beautiful.

3. As we navigate Keith's mental health journey, I've found myself thinking of Cain lately.

He's a guy feeling the pressures of being an older brother, and all of a sudden, he gets the news that his offering wasn't accepted like his younger brother's was. We're not told why not, and we don't know if Cain ultimately knew why or not. He's pissed (and I don't blame him one bit), and now we do see God come into the picture. In essence, God says, "It's one mistake. Do the next right thing, and we'll move forward from here."

Yet Cain is still reeling from the rejection and feels, "What the...did I do wrong?!" He appears to need a detailed closure before he can move forward. Again, I do not blame him one bit. He takes matters into his own hands and thinks, "I think I burned a bridge, but let me just make sure of it," and takes Abel's life. I've been there. I can think of a time when I thought I burned a bridge, so I did other things to make **sure** I burned the bridge. And then Cain's left wandering, terrified that people will kill him. God assures him no one will and marks him. He marries and has a son, Enoch. Not the Enoch who walked with God, like I had hoped, just some random person. I just have to ask,

Was there ever redemption for Cain? What was his ending? Did he ever get to understand that **he** wasn't his sin: God just wanted to **wipe his sin off of him**?

Throughout this mental health journey, I've been pondering, "Are we Cain in this
story? Are we missing something? Are we being marked for safekeeping and then getting to wander our lives away?"

We started counseling last week, and I think it will be really helpful. I'm hoping it will be a mix of healing from the past and gaining tools to help in the future. I know that God is in the process of redeeming our lives. It just feels like we've been in the desert a long dang time, and I'm exhausted!

****

Life finally began to settle down in the fall of 2023. Things looked different, for sure, but we finally began moving forward. As Keith was healing, I found my mental health starting to wave a white flag. I'd been through a lot, and I needed rest. I was so thankful Keith was able to step up to the task. His relationship with Lucas had blossomed, and it was beautiful to watch. I remember one time we were at a park, and there was a swing where both parent and child could swing together, facing each other. Lucas LOVED doing that with Keith and was so upset when we left. As exhausting as that meltdown was - because the little man was tired, it was a long one - it was also adorable, because he loved that face-to-face experience with his daddy and couldn't fathom its ending.

****

As this chapter comes to an end, I have to think about the song that closed out our wedding ceremony - "Somebody Like You" by Keith Urban[4]. As I mentioned before, Keith Urban was my favorite singer in high school, and I made sure to watch every interview he did. I learned that he had made some poor choices, and if he had been famous at that time, he would have completely ruined his fame journey. However, he figured out how to rise above the challenges to become the success he is today. In "Somebody Like You", Keith is honest about his journey, and with eyes fresh with gratitude, he looks forward to a new and full life.

I found my CD with that song recently, and it feels like that song is a mirror into the life we're leading. I love that Lucas also enjoys the song; we listen to it regularly on the way to preschool, both singing it at the top of our lungs. It's even better when we can have the windows down.

To quote the song: "It sure feels good to finally feel the way I do...I wanna love somebody like you." Where we're at right now feels good, and I am so proud to say that I can love someone like (my!) Keith.

NOTES

[1] Brené Brown. 2021. *Atlas of the Heart.* New York Random House.

[2] Rachel Held Evans. 2015. *Searching for Sunday : Loving, Leaving, and Finding the Church.* Nashville, Tennessee: Nelson Books.

[3] Wilkerson, Isabel. 2021. *CASTE: The International Bestseller.* S.L.: Penguin Books.

[4] Urban, Keith . 2002. *Somebody like You.* Album. Nashville: Capitol Records.

Twelve

Tender Shoots

Each January 1st from 2020-2023, I faced the start of the new year optimistically. We still use a paper calendar that hangs up on the wall, so each time I could get rid of a whole calendar, I felt a weight fall off. "This next year will be different," I'd think to myself, only to be blindsided again. I felt like I was in the ocean during a storm; each time I'd drag myself up from the hit of a huge wave, the next massive one would sneak up and knock me over again.

At the start of 2024, I felt both weary as well as wary. We had been attending a home church that was wonderful for our situation; the leaders knew what we had been through and were very supportive. However, Lucas was the only little one present, and we knew he needed to be around peers; we eventually decided to start attending a new church.

I mentioned in a previous chapter that I've never been great with expectations. As an idealist, I see what could be and will it to become reality. You can probably guess my track record with this method! I was not enthusiastic about our next endeavor at all. I cried on the last Sunday we attended the home church. I was apprehensive, less than optimistic, and so. dang. tired. I told people I was heading into this new adventure with expectations less than an inch high.

I ended up being pleasantly surprised! Here are some ways I felt God move through the people at the new church:

Intention - On our very first Sunday, the senior pastor flagged us down after the service because he saw us BEFORE the service and knew we were new. On our second Sunday there, he greeted Keith by name.

Gentleness - I joined a small group with a focus on mentoring and after sharing bits of the last few years, I wasn't pushed away. I was surrounded by warmth and a willingness to walk this journey with me.

Kindness - I helped out with an event in the spring and was given a gift card as a thank you! So unnecessary, yet so sweet! Also, the way the volunteers work with Lucas melts my heart!

Carried by structure - Some churches smother their congregation with structure. Other churches completely disregard structure. This church seems to use structure as a springboard to the spontaneity of the Holy Spirit. It feels like a weight off somehow. I won't get lost in the hustle and bustle, but I also won't be suffocated. It feels like a healthy anchor.

****

In 2024, I was finally able to drag myself out of the proverbial waters, sit on the sand, and catch a breath. I've been able to feel the warm sand on my feet, concentrate on the grains of sand slipping between my fingers, and let the sun begin to dry me off.

In 2024, I thought a lot about a social media post I wrote back in 2023:

"Last week, out of the blue, I dreamed about Mama two nights in a row. It frustrated me because it took the dull ache of her absence and made it a fresh sting again.

The dream led me to reminiscing again. The main memory that persisted was when Keith and I picked her up in Philly a week before our wedding. The plan was for her to land early in the evening, but as flights go, we found ourselves wandering bleary-eyed through the airport at 1am. I was wondering how I was going to find her because she changed hairstyles A LOT.

Were we even in the right place? How would we get in touch with each other if there were issues?

We were walking along, our eyes peeled, and finally somewhat close to us, I thought I saw her and turned suddenly. I was so focused that I didn't hear Keith ask where I was

going. I called her name two or three times, and it was her!

Crisis averted.

I think that memory holds significance for today, too. I'm really emotionally exhausted and am trying to figure out how to get my energy back. I feel like this memory is showing me that I am trying to look to the past to solve my current problems. Like me tuning out Keith in my focused pursuit of Mama, I'm tuning out God in my focused pursuit of things in the past.

Unlike the memory, Mama's not going to acknowledge me because...she can't. The energy and zest for life back in 2016-2018 (which seem to be the magic years I'm striving to get back to emotionally)...are in the past.

I need to figure out how to use what's in the present to get me to a more energized place. I'm thankful for the gentle and kind ways God shows us the ways we need to walk in."

∗∗∗∗∗∗∗∗∗∗

In this last chapter of my book, I want to revisit the previous chapters and reflect on how I've gained clarity since 2019. I've not gained 100% crystal-clear clarity; I feel like the man in whose eyes Jesus put mud as a way to heal him, found in Mark 8. The man needed a double dose of mud, because after the first time, men looked like walking trees. I'll just assume that my clarity is of the "walking trees" kind and trust that crystal-clear clarity will come when I'm face-to-face with Jesus.

Writing Chapter 1 was an eye-opener for me. I learned that my anxiety wasn't from trying to stay ahead of the expectations of the world, so the world wouldn't crush me. I learned that my anxiety stemmed from hefting around the discomfort other people had of me and my physical and emotional uniqueness. Writing the first chapter gave me the courage to begin to hand over the discomfort to whom it belonged - to the people who were actually uncomfortable with me. It is no longer my burden to bear. The sense of freedom that has been emerging since writing Chapter 1 is palpable.

In the midst of writing Chapter 1, I turned 38. I had my first ever moment of "midlife crisis" when I said to myself, "Here's to the next 38 years!...Wait, that brings me to 76. Is it possible that my life is (more than) half over?!" I realized that I wanted the next half of my life to look different from the first half.

I've heard that we carry all the previous versions of ourselves in the current version of ourselves. As I reflected on that, I had to think that when I turned 18, along with many friends and other people in the area, I took advantage of the opportunities that came my way. I threw myself into my studies and graduated from college cum laude in 3.5 years with a major in German Education, a minor in Linguistics, and an honors thesis written in German. My advisor even looked at me, surprised and asked how I accomplished all of that in that short timeframe. I didn't know how, but I felt on top of the world. I was a globe-trotter; I lived in Germany for a year and went on three trips to The Land of Transformation. I got my Master's Degree and wrote another thesis. I have a satisfying job, I'm in a solid marriage, which is ironically a tribute to the past few years, and I have a wonderful five-year-old son. Society tends to call that a successful life, and I agree. However...

The version of me that is younger than 18 has been waving the white flag for all of these years. To borrow a word I saw on social media, she is "exhausterwhelmulated" - the awful combination of exhaustion, overwhelm, and overstimulation. She is tired of performing, of carrying the burden of others' discomfort, of being told that hard times make her stronger. She would argue that she doesn't need to be stronger; she needs comfort, encouragement, a place to lay down her fears, a place to rest. She needs to be accepted for the person she is, not forced to be the person she "should be." She's tired of "shoulding herself."

Writing Chapter 1 has been a vital key to unlocking the freedom my younger self needs.

****

My journey with Jesus began with a good foundation as mentioned in Chapters 2 and 5, and it brought me far. However, I don't think just that foundation alone would have brought me from 2019-2024. I absolutely need to give a shout-out to the BEMA podcast, which I referenced in Chapter 2. Keith and I discovered it in the beginning of 2020, and it has been a faith-saver. This podcast looks at the Bible from the Jewish perspective because as we all too often forget to think about, the Bible wasn't written to the Western world! It was written by Jews for Jews.

This does not mean the Bible is not for Westerners; it simply means that the Western view of the Bible is only part of the story. We need the "Eastern" view to make our understanding of God's plan for the world more complete. One of BEMA's mottos is "Trust the story." Can we believe that no matter what is going on in our lives and in the world that God is good? That God is for us? That He can turn awful experiences into moments that give Him glory?

One of the ways in which I have benefited from this podcast is the viewpoint that the God of the New Testament is the exact same God of the Old Testament! My church experience has always highlighted the "discrepancy" that God was different in the Old and New Testaments, and now that Jesus is here, we can completely disregard the God of the Old Testament. Through the BEMA lens, however, I've noticed that God is love all throughout Scripture! The Old Testament has been redeemed for me, and I can see God's love in the ancient stories.

Receiving this new lens through which to view God, I've received more permission to breathe. To go easier on myself. This doesn't mean I should be lax and keep sinning because grace is there to catch me. To quote the group Tenth Avenue North, this lens allows us to view God as a parent who says to us when we slip up, "Let's get up and try again."[1] Sin isn't IN us; it's a decision we make, and if we do the next right thing, all is well again.

Along with BEMA, I discovered *The Chosen* series in 2022. At first, I was pretty wary because Christian TV tends to be cheesy at best, but I was completely wrong! The restorative way in which Jesus lived is highlighted in every interaction; He met chaos with calm, snark with sincerity, and traps with trust. Watching *The Chosen* makes a life of faith and following Jesus seem doable. Not easy by any stretch of the imagination, but it's also not a complicated formula. I would argue that the series shows us where we, as believers, make things difficult.

Over these past few years, I have been so thankful for creators who bring the Bible to life in fresh and exciting ways.

****

The chapters about The Land of Transformation leave my heart with a never-ending ache. I don't know if there is any clarity here. These chapters are the main part of the last few years where closure eludes me. Would I feel more closure had I been able to attend Mama's funeral and comfort those who felt like family? Would I feel more closure had my other friend not died five weeks after Mama? This other friend was a huge support in setting up the 501c3, as she had also started a 501c3. She had given me so many documents that were lawyer-approved and permitted me to make them applicable to my situation. This other friend would have absolutely kept spurring me on; maybe she could have spoken up for me when searing grief sapped me of words. It's all just speculation, I guess.

The last time I was in The Land of Transformation was in 2018, and the last time I was in regular contact with friends over there was in 2020. I feel guilty that I stopped the contact because I was overwhelmed with the pandemic and wanted to help people around me. I didn't have the energy to think about people thousands of miles away from me. It's one of those lessons of "No one can do everything, but everyone can do something." If I hadn't set boundaries, I would have run myself into the ground thinking that I had to do everything. But it still hurts. I still hate the various inequalities that present themselves between our two countries.

I've also changed my philosophy of going to developing countries. I don't want to go with an organization anymore because I don't believe organizations provide long-term good to these countries. If these organizations did come up with long-term solutions, they would eventually work themselves out of a job. That was our organization's initial goal: we wanted to help the ministry become self-sufficient so that the staff and kids wouldn't need us anymore. The only organization I can think of that "knows, goes, shows, blows" (from Chapter 4), is Global Disciples. The Westerners empower people to serve in their own countries and come back only to implement new technology, to encourage the churches, and to assist in pressing matters. That's it. Otherwise, it's the local people running the local church. It is amazing.

I've heard (and experienced) that the Western "mission industry" is essentially a money racket. If the industry is really that successful in the way it runs, why are there still people who haven't heard the good news of Jesus? Where is all that money even going? Are there good accountability systems in place? Might there also be a hint of the "White Savior" mindset? The need to feel needed, so I feel like I'm significant?

If I ever go back to another developing place, my goal would be to pump as much money as possible into the local economy. Then

I would be meeting real people with real needs and impacting their economy in a real way.

****

I'm not denying that God has worked through mission organizations. I'm simply asking missionaries to be honest with themselves and ponder, "Who got the most benefit from my time abroad? Was it the people I came to serve, or was it me?" It's a hard question to ask ourselves. I know I'd asked myself that about my time in The Land of Transformation several times, but because I had such a good relationship with Mama that spanned seven years and held a lot of raw and real conversations with her, I felt I could trust that she actually wanted me as a part of her vision. In Chapter 7, I talked about sitting at people's feet and listening to their stories and how that act of humility truly shows people you care. That was essentially the same posture I took with Mama, and she appreciated it.

I remember her telling me that the ministry needed some supplies, and she gave me all of the specifics. I said, "You do what you need to do, and we'll support you the best way we can." She said, "I am so glad to work with you. So many Americans in the past have questioned my needs and have viewed my requests as challenges to say 'no' to." I never understood that mindset. Why do Americans feel the need to be at the top of everything they are involved with? I, along with most of the board members, was happy to serve her because we trusted that her connection to God and His vision was secure. I guess I just need to lay down any unnecessary responsibility I feel and trust, as I said in Chapter 8, that I truly haven't grasped the depth of the promise that the last will be first. These dear ones are seen, known, held, and loved by the One who loves them the very most.

****

Bringing the conversation back to the US, I have to think about the way Christians tend to apologize. Writing Chapter 9 reminded me that we don't do a great job at it; if we even admit we do something wrong, that tends to be the extent of the apology. The BEMA podcast has outlined the Hebrew way to apologize.[2] The process is as follows:

To admit there is wrongdoing - confession

1. To acknowledge that your actions caused a negative impact on the person you wronged directly (if possible) as well as anyone indirectly impacted.
2. To make any possible restitution - to the point where the wronged person says, "OK, it wasn't THAT bad!'
3. To share a plan with others on how you are not going to do the same thing again
4. To change behavior - essentially walking the walk of Steps 1-4

We don't hear that preached from too many pulpits, do we? I think it's because the process is so dang hard, and pastors might wonder if they will have a job after that message. I get it. The difficulty doesn't excuse our bad behavior, though. Where does our behavior need to make the amends that our mouths so easily uttered?

****

It's the humility vs hubris discussion. Our "hubris" can't fathom that we've done anything wrong; that's why the definition is "*dangerous* overconfidence." It takes so much probing on our part, and it's no wonder that King David had to ask God to search his heart to see if there's anything offensive in him (Psalm 139:22). David knew he needed an extra pair of eyes to hone in on the areas he would gladly skip over.

The process hurts, plain and simple. Not just emotionally, but depending on the area of weakness, it might even hurt physically, as well. I remember talking to a friend about this process one time, and she reminded me, "Michelle, God doesn't come in with a machete, swinging blindly and randomly at anything that moves. He comes in with a double-edged sword, desiring only to make the smallest cut necessary, so it hurts as little as possible." Referencing Chapter 2's mention of the author of *The Shack*, God judges our areas of sin and weakness as a doctor, wanting only to heal and never to harm.

True repentance seems so scary, but it can be really easy. I've been trying to practice it with Lucas, and it often looks like:

I'm sorry I... Can you forgive me? Next time, I'll...

Sometimes he'll initiate the process with me when he's done something wrong. It's a beautiful thing to be vulnerable, and I believe it makes relationships that much stronger.

****

The content in Chapter 9 also makes me wonder how many people understand the difference between "being nice" and "being kind." "Being nice" just requires you to say flowery things and cliches so old and dusty that you choke on them and cough and sputter when someone says them to you. "Being kind" requires action.

Before dying of COVID in the fall of 2021, my school's superintendent transformed the atmosphere of our school. Before him, upper administration denied teachers a contract and union, and I remember in my first year how one teacher told me that half of the faculty were on anxiety meds. When the new superintendent came on board in my second year at the school, there was so much fear and trembling, and when he invited teachers to talk to him about problems they were facing, there was so much skepticism. Yet, I remember one friend telling me, "Two weeks after I spoke with him, I saw my problems being addressed!" He willingly paved the way for a contract and a union for us, plus he made it possible for part-time teachers - like me! - to receive benefits! I've never heard of any employer giving part-timers benefits. We all miss him terribly. What is this now...the third death I've been impacted by in five years? I'm so freaking tired of death!

But that's kindness - the willingness to get your hands dirty and to bend yourself down and work with people you actually wouldn't have to work with. I've heard that "Kindness is when someone lacks strength and you give them some of yours." Kindness is sacrifice; it's humility in action, thinking of others more than yourself.

****

My reflections on apologies and niceness vs. kindness for Chapter 9 flow very easily into my reflections about Chapter 10. I'm still finding traces of Chapter 10 in my life that have me feeling one of two ways. Depending on the day, I either feel haunted and discouraged by it all, or I find myself motivated to ask Jesus for help. I have actually come face-to-face with one of the traces, and the result was surprising. This person shared her feelings about the church we had left, and it was eerily similar to my story. She presented something to the leadership team that she found concerning, and they didn't take her seriously. They actually said more harmful things to her than they did to me, and have actually told her not to come to church events anymore.

Before I knew it, I found myself empathizing with her and telling her that she wasn't the problem! I couldn't believe what was happening in my heart, but as I was thinking about it later, the reason dawned on me. When I feel validated and when the other person is honest and shows humility, my heart opens. All of the feelings vanished where she was concerned. That's not to say we've become friends, but I can at least be genuinely friendly with her.

****

A few months later, I had another chance to test out my theory of "validation + vulnerability = healing" with a different trace of Chapter 10. It wasn't a direct conversation, though; this person was speaking in front of a group. As she was sharing her story, the moment came where I thought I would get to experience empathy, and I actually shifted eagerly in my seat, waiting for the moment I had felt in the first experience. I quickly realized, though, that it would never come. This person was neither humble nor completely honest. I felt anger and knew I needed to talk to Jesus.

One of the things I love about *The Chosen* is how easy it was for people to talk to Jesus, when He was available. This gave me a renewed sense of gratitude for the opportunity to talk with Him whenever we want. I've actually begun imagining myself talking to the Jesus from the series. I honestly wonder how many minds the actor Jonathan Roumie (Jesus) has occupied for this very reason! He's just that great at his role.

I'm awful at imagining scenery and envisioning the garments we'd be wearing in Jesus' time if I were talking to the actual person of Jesus, but one thing I know for sure. I would find every moment possible not to wear anything on my head, such as the long piece of material the women wore over their heads in *The Chosen*. I hate any kind of headwear, and I can imagine Jesus winking at me and coming to my defense at times.

Here's what I believe our conversation would sound like. Where you see "...," that's me shielding you from the strong language I often use while talking to Jesus. He already knows what we're thinking; we might as well just say it. However, if this would make you uncomfortable, please feel free to skip this section.

Me (sits down in a huff): Ugggghhhh, I'm so...angry!

Jesus: What's going on?

Me: Why do people feel like they can pretend to be perfect? What do they get out of it?

Jesus: Why do you care so strongly about how other people carry themselves?

Me: Because it hurts people! It's judgmental, it's dishonest, and it shows other people that they shouldn't be their true selves either. People often get excluded if they can't live up to arbitrary standards.

Jesus: Have you been hurt by people like that?

Me: Where... have You been the last five years? Of course, I've been hurt by people like that!

Jesus (thinking for a bit): Are you sure *you're* being totally honest with me right now?

Me (exasperated): Yes! No? ...I don't know!

Jesus: Has it just been these last few years that you've had these strong feelings?

Me: Are you...kidding me right now?! I thought You were all-knowing; of course this hasn't been the only time!

Jesus (takes my hands, looks me in the eyes, and says): "Let's take some breaths before we continue." (We breathe together)

Jesus: I wonder if you think I'm teasing you. (*I nod*). I know that you have had a number of people in your life who like to say things and push your buttons to get a rise out of you. I don't do that. If I say things that make you feel frantic and trapped, it's because I'm inviting you to an uncomfortable place. I'm not sending you there alone, though. I'm there, too.

Me: Why...do I get the invitation?! Why don't the people who are hurting others get the invitation?!

Jesus (takes a deep breath): You know, the only person you can control is yourself. Contrary to popular belief, *I'm* not even in control of you. I'm in charge of every situation, but I don't control people's actions.

Me: Well, honestly, sometimes I feel like You're doing an awfully...job at being in charge.

Jesus (wryly): Yeah, and you'd do so much better.

Me: Ugh, I know, I'm sorry, I'm just so...angry!

Jesus: And the uncomfortable place I'm inviting you to is where we explore your feelings more.

Me: Ugh, fiiiiiiiiiiine.

Jesus: You've explored the idea that you still carry all the younger versions of yourself around. Is the anger coming from who you are currently?

Me: No, the current me is so....tired; she can't fathom being upset at insecure people. It probably comes from my youth group years when I got excluded a lot.

Jesus: What did you need at that age?

Me: ....revenge! To see people held accountable for their actions! To hold people accountable myself!

Jesus: What would that accountability look like?

Me: To see what they did to me done to them!

Jesus (one eyebrow raised): So, you want to hurt people?

Me: No! Yes? ...stop twisting my words!

Jesus: I'm pretty sure you're doing the twisting here. And it sounds like that's your anger talking. Remember that anger is fear's bodyguard. What is your anger guarding?

Me: Ugh, can we be done here?

Jesus: We can stop this conversation, sure. I won't force you to do anything you don't want to do. I will say, though, that we're getting close to something.

Me: ....! Fiiiiiiiine!

Jesus: Can I tell you what I'm seeing? Maybe this will make it easier.

Me: You mean this conversation could have been over ten minutes ago if you would have just done that right off the bat?!

Jesus: Theoretically. But I don't lecture. I like the back-and-forth.

Me: Whatever, I'm listening.

Jesus: I see that teenager in you who is thirsting for revenge. Even more so, though, I see you at an even younger age doing everything she can to fit in, so she doesn't stand out any more than she already does. She plays the game of life by the rules and wins some with people and loses some with people. When she loses, she gets disoriented, "Wait, they cheated. They weren't supposed to act that way, but they did, and they still won? How does that make any sense?" The younger you still plays the game by the rules because she knows that's what she needs to do to survive, but she is still confused by the discrepancy of "what is" and "what should be."

Me: I'm still confused by that discrepancy!

Jesus: I know you are. Let me remind you that I see the injustices done in this world far more clearly than you do. I can promise you that the injustices do not have the final say. And while I ask you to do your part in making the world a more just place, I'm not asking you to take on all responsibility. That's way too heavy for you. You have my permission to "stay in your lane." I'm not asking you to do more than what's in front of you - to act justly, to love mercy, and to walk humbly with Me (Micah 6:8). The people who exclude others will need to repent, just like you do in other areas. And I do offer them this same invitation I've offered you. You all are on your own journey. You're all... in some ways and saints in others. And I love the whole lot of you.

(We hug; end scene)

Just to let you all know, I went into this dialogue thinking I knew what Jesus and I were going to say; we've had many of these conversations after all. In reality, however, there were real-time interruptions from Jesus while I was writing this that took the conversation in a different way and led to real tears. He's full of surprises!

Jesus has also shared with me that if I want to get out of the rat race, if I want to rid myself of any drama, then I need to go lower. Lower in the sense of bowing down at Jesus' feet and asking Him for help. Lower, where it's so much clearer what matters in the spiritual realm. Lower, to hang out with the vulnerable populations because that's where He is. That's not to say the lights and loudness of a Sunday morning are a bad thing. Jesus is present in those moments, but He doesn't live there. He lives in the realm of needs, of humility, and of humble surroundings. He lives in the obvious imperfections of humanity with the goal to make things incrementally better with His presence. He's never in a rush; He's always up for a meal and a laugh. He doesn't play favorites; there's no "winner" in His Kingdom. I love these lines from the song by We Are Messengers:

We all need the same medicine.
We all need another second chance.
There's no first in line at the foot of the Cross.
(We are Made in the Image of God)[3]

These lines are choking me up even now as I'm writing. It's not about being first. It's not about being the most important. It's about being willing to give all of your life to Jesus to see what He wants to do with it. Some people are given one talent, some two, and some five (Matthew 25). Note: the person with one talent didn't get berated because he had less than the others. He was reprimanded because he didn't do anything with it. If we spend our lives trying to be someone else because we hate what we've been given, that's what grieves Jesus. When we wriggle out of the heavy armor of hubris and put on the much lighter robe of humility, that's where He is able to move.

****

When I think about "going lower" in the context of Chapter 11, I think to myself, "Haven't we gone low enough?! Is there anything lower than the depths of Sheol?!" Then Jesus calms me down and shows me that "going lower" in this circumstance is an act of rolling up my sleeves and getting to the work of walking out the aftermath of a miracle.

Walking out a miracle is hard work. We sing constantly about how Jesus is the Waymaker, who has fought every battle we are facing, and will always come out victorious. All of that is very true, but...

What happens after the victory is won and the spoils are collected?

A friend showed me a post on social media, about miracles being hard work. When Jesus healed the paralytic and the blind, guess what? They had to get new jobs. When He stopped the woman's bleeding, she had to wrestle her way back into society - how do you prove you were healed from THAT?! When He told the woman caught in adultery that He doesn't condemn her and urged her to leave her life of sin, she had to learn to walk the confusing walk of freedom.

We don't talk enough about the aftermath of miracles. It's long. It's confusing. It's tedious. It messes with you; it kinda makes you want to go back to the way things were - think the Israelites in the desert. It's simply not flashy or instantaneous enough for the Western Church. We want the change and the results of the change, but we don't want to go on that journey from A to B.

I think that's one reason for my exhaustion over these past few years. Jesus isn't just our Victor; He's Emmanuel - with us on the journey, however long it takes.

****

This journey after the miracle has been relatively stable, and I couldn't be more thankful. At the time of this writing, Keith has decreased his medication dose twice with the OK from his doctor, and we haven't seen any setbacks! It's been a huge gift. Keith's latest work environment has provided him more time to rest, get projects done around the house, and find new hobbies.

Though I'm tired, I can still find enough energy to be amazed at how God has kept our marriage and family intact. Going through this mental health journey has shown Keith and me how to be more open with each other. In counseling, we discovered ways in which we had been trying to protect each other from things in life because we didn't know if the other person could handle it. Early on, it was good that I shielded Keith from some of my emotions, but as we became more stable, we needed to become more vulnerable with each other. That realization was eye-opening, and ultimately, very helpful.

The relationship between Keith and Lucas has also blossomed so much. They are currently involved in an outdoor-themed group through our church, and that has been a great experience for both of them. They've had a campout, a car race, and they've gone fishing. Lucas often likes to tag along on errands with Keith, and I love seeing the two of them walk out the door with their baseball caps, ready to explore the world.

After coming out of the heaviest part of the mental health journey, Lucas seemed OK at first, aside from the occasional, "Will Daddy come back?" when Keith would leave for some time. That question always gutted me. After about a year, though, we saw signs that he might need to work through some emotions. I had read something about anxiety, and if the parents can, they should give their child as much time as possible to get the emotions out before moving to the next part of the day. I did that with Lucas one day, intentionally setting a timer for 30 minutes and waiting to see what would happen. After about ten minutes of what I expected to hear, Lucas' cries turned to, "I want Daddy!" That was a major revelation.

We were fortunate enough to find a play therapy location close to our house, and Lucas loved it. Miss Melanie was perfect for him; she loved Jesus, and she was extremely calm, so attuned to what Lucas needed. The idea behind play therapy is that it is child-led, and the therapist follows along using different strategies. After the first session, I asked if we should help clean up the room, and she said, "Nope! That's like stuffing your emotions back down and undoing all the work you just did." Amazing. Lucas had weekly appointments for about three months, and the therapy strategies were successful! It was a reminder to me that you can keep drama from becoming trauma if you can deal with it as close to the event as possible.

××*×*×*×*

As I'm about to wrap this book up, I have to think of author and professor Kate Bowler, who became well-known at some point after receiving a stage 4 cancer diagnosis. She didn't just survive; she is thriving. She is a successful author, podcast host, and speaker. At one point, someone asked her if she would give up all this success if it meant she wouldn't have received the cancer diagnosis. Without hesitation, she said Absolutely. This success is great and all, but if she could have done without the cancer and lived another kind of life, she would have done that in a heartbeat.

I resonated with that so much. Yes, I've learned and grown a lot. Yes, I've been given the opportunity to write a book, which I've wanted to do for years, but I would give all of it up to have Mama with me again and to have Keith be free of mental health stuff. The silver lining is great, but some days, I feel like my original dream was better. These last few years have taught me so much about surrender. I feel like some Christians think "surrender" indicates that a person has reached a state of nirvana, but I disagree. I feel like "surrender" is the beginning of the journey to our one messy and beautiful life with Jesus. "Surrender" means you lay down the outcome and the end of all things and willingly walk the current journey one step at a time, "trusting the Story," as the BEMA hosts would say.

****

I think an appropriate ending to this book is to say that my little family has plans to visit dear friends in South Dakota this summer, and Keith has agreed to fly - for the very first time. Lucas is going to start kindergarten next year; he's ready to fly into this new world of "big kid" school. Thinking about having regular time off from motherhood each day makes my spirit fly. I can't wait to see what new endeavors will come my way, will come OUR way in this next season of life. Whatever comes our way, I rest in the fact that we are seen, known, held, and loved. As are you, dear reader. Thanks for accompanying me on this journey.

NOTES

[1] Tenth Avenue North. 2019. *Greater than All My Regrets.* Album. Provident Label Group.

[2] Solomon, Marty. "Forgiveness." Produced by Brent Bilings. *BEMA Podcast.* November 14, 2024. Podcast, 39:48.

[3] We are Messengers. 2020. *Image of God*. Album. Nashville: Curb/Word Entertainment.

Michelle lives in Pennsylvania with her husband and son. She feels deeply and loves fiercely. Her mission is for others to know that they can have the courage to be the person God created them to be without fearing what others think.

Book Summary

Michelle Martin's story begins with difficult health challenges that lead her to unexpected places, where she encounters a most remarkable and inspirational woman. In this book, Martin changes as she is faced with profound grief, relationship challenges, and tragedies, yet this is not a depressing memoir, nor is it one filled with superficial platitudes. Martin tells a love story, about God who speaks to us in all kinds of circumstances, and she is not afraid to ask the deep questions or look beyond the surface. This book will challenge you to think, to see things from a new perspective, and to grow in your own journey.